William Shakespeare was born in Stratford-upon-Avon in April 1564, and his birth is traditionally celebrated on April 23. The facts of his life, known from surviving documents, are sparse. He was one of eight children born to John Shakespeare, a merchant of some standing in his community. William probably went to the King's New School in Stratford, but he had no university education. In November 1582, at the age of eighteen, he married Anne Hathaway, eight years his senior, who was pregnant with their first child, Susanna. She was born on May 26, 1583. Twins, a boy, Hamnet (who would die at age eleven), and a girl, Judith, were born in 1585. By 1592 Shakespeare had gone to London, working as an actor and already known as a playwright. A rival dramatist, Robert Greene, referred to him as "an upstart crow, beautified with our feathers." Shakespeare became a principal shareholder and playwright of the successful acting troupe, the Lord Chamberlain's Men (later, under James I, called the King's Men). In 1599 the Lord Chamberlain's Men built and occupied the Globe Theatre in Southwark near the Thames River. Here many of Shakespeare's plays were performed by the most famous actors of his time, including Richard Burbage, Will Kempe, and Robert Armin. In addition to his 37 plays, Shakespeare had a hand in others, including *Sir Thomas More* and *The Two Noble Kinsmen*, and he wrote poems, including *Venus and Adonis* and *The Rape of Lucrece*. His 154 sonnets were published, probably without his authorization, in 1609. In 1611 or 1612 he gave up his lodgings in London and devoted more and more of his time to retirement in Stratford, though he continued writing such plays as *The Tempest* and *Henry VIII* until about 1613. He died on April 23, 1616, and was buried in Holy Trinity Church, Stratford. No collected edition of his plays was published during his lifetime, but in 1623 two members of his acting company, John Heminges and Henry Condell, published the great collection now called the First Folio.

William Shakespeare

RICHARD II

Edited by
David Bevington
and
David Scott Kastan

BANTAM CLASSIC

RICHARD II

A Bantam Book / published by arrangement with Pearson Education, Inc.

PUBLISHING HISTORY

Scott, Foresman edition published January 1980
Bantam edition, with newly edited text and substantially revised, edited,
and amplified notes, introduction, and other materials / February 1988
Bantam reissue with updated notes, introduction,
and other materials / February 2006

Published by Bantam Dell
A Division of Random House, Inc.
New York, New York

Valuable advice on staging matters has been provided by Richard Hosley
Collations checked by Eric Rasmussen
Additional editorial assistance by Claire McEachern

Book design by Virginia Norey

Library of Congress Catalog Card Number: 87-23198

ISBN-10: 0-553-21303-2
ISBN-13: 978-0-553-21303-4

Printed in the United States of America
Published simultaneously in Canada
OPM   16 15 14 13 12 11 10 9 8 7

CONTENTS

INTRODUCTION

Richard II (c. 1595–1596) is the first play in Shakespeare's great four-play historical saga, or tetralogy, that continues with the two parts of *Henry IV* (c. 1596–1598) and concludes with *Henry V* (1599). In this, his second, tetralogy, Shakespeare dramatizes the beginnings of the great conflict called the Wars of the Roses, having already dramatized the conclusion of that civil war in his earlier tetralogy on Henry VI and Richard III (c. 1589–1594). Both sequences move from an outbreak of civil faction to the eventual triumph of political stability. Together they constitute the story of England's long century of political turmoil from the 1390s until Henry Tudor's victory over Richard III in 1485. Yet Shakespeare chose to tell the two halves of this chronicle in reverse order. His culminating statement about kingship in *Henry V* focuses on the earlier historical period, on the education and kingly success of Prince Hal.

With *Richard II*, then, Shakespeare turns to the events that had launched England's century of crisis. These events were still fresh and relevant to Elizabethan minds. Richard and Bolingbroke's contest for the English crown provided a sobering example of political wrongdoing and, at least by implication, a rule for political right conduct. One prominent reason for studying history, to an Elizabethan, was to avoid the errors of the past. The relevance of such historical analogy was, in fact, vividly underscored some six years after Shakespeare wrote the play: in 1601, followers of the Earl of Essex commissioned Shakespeare's acting company to perform a revived play about Richard II on the eve of what was to be an abortive rebellion, perhaps with the intention of inciting a riot. Whether the play was Shakespeare's is not certain, but it seems likely. The acting company was ultimately exonerated, but not before Queen

Elizabeth concluded that she was being compared to Richard II. When he wrote the play, Shakespeare presumably did not know that it would be used for such a purpose, but he must have known that the overthrow of Richard II was, in any case, a controversial subject because of its potential use as a precedent for rebellion. The scene of Richard's deposition (4.1) was considered so provocative by Elizabeth's government that it was censored in the printed quartos of Shakespeare's play during the Queen's lifetime.

In view of the startling relevance of this piece of history to Shakespeare's own times, then, what are the rights and wrongs of Richard's deposition, and to what extent can political lessons be drawn from Shakespeare's presentation?

To begin with, we should not underestimate Richard's attractive qualities, as a man and even as a king. Throughout the play, Richard is consistently more impressive and majestic in appearance than his rival, Bolingbroke. Richard fascinates us with his verbal sensitivity, his poetic insight, and his dramatic self-consciousness. He eloquently expounds a sacramental view of kingship, according to which "Not all the water in the rough rude sea / Can wash the balm off from an anointed king" (3.2.54–5). Bolingbroke can depose Richard but can never capture the aura of majesty Richard possesses; Bolingbroke may succeed politically but only at the expense of desecrating an idea. Richard is much more interesting to us as a man than Bolingbroke, more capable of grief, more tender in his personal relationships, and more in need of being understood. Indeed, a major factor in Richard's tragedy is the conflict between his public role (wherein he sees himself as divinely appointed, almost superhuman) and his private role (wherein he is emotionally dependent and easily hurt). He confuses what the medieval and Renaissance world knew as the king's "two bodies," the sacramental body of kingship, which is eternal, and the human body of a single occupant of the throne, whose frail mortal condition is subject to time and fortune. Richard's failure to perceive and to act wisely on this difference is part of his tragic predicament, but his increasing insight, through suffering, into the truth of the distinction is also part of his spiritual growth. His dilemma, however poignantly individual, lies at the heart of kingship. Richard is thus very much a king. Although he sometimes indulges in childish sentimentality, at his best he is superbly refined, perceptive, and poetic.

These qualities notwithstanding, Richard is an incompetent ruler, compared with the man who supplants him. Richard himself confesses to the prodigal expense of "too great a court." In order to raise funds, he has been obliged to "farm our royal realm"; that is, to sell for ready cash the right of collecting taxes to individual courtiers, who are then free to extort what the market will bear (1.4.43–5). Similarly, Richard proposes to issue "blank charters" (line 48) to his minions, who will then be authorized to fill in the amount of tax to be paid by any hapless subject. These abuses were infamous to Elizabethan audiences as symbols of autocratic misgovernment. No less heinous is Richard's seizure of the dukedom of Lancaster from his cousin Bolingbroke. Although Richard does receive the consent of his Council to banish Bolingbroke because of the divisiveness of the quarrel between him and Mowbray, the King violates the very idea of inheritance of property when he takes away Bolingbroke's title and lands. And, as his uncle the Duke of York remonstrates, Richard's own right to the throne depends on that idea of due inheritance. By offending against the most sacred concepts of order and degree, he teaches others to rebel.

Richard's behavior even prior to the commencement of the play arouses suspicion. The nature of his complicity in the death of his uncle Thomas of Woodstock, Duke of Gloucester, is perhaps never entirely clear, and Gloucester may have given provocation. Indeed, one can sympathize with the predicament of a young ruler prematurely thrust into the center of power by the untimely death of his father, the crown prince, now having to cope with an array of worldly-wise, advice-giving uncles. Nevertheless, Richard is unambiguously guilty of murder in the eyes of Gloucester's widow, while her brother-in-law John of Gaunt, Duke of Lancaster, assumes that Richard has caused Gloucester's death, "the which if wrongfully / Let heaven revenge" (1.2.39–40).

Apparently, too, Gaunt's son Bolingbroke believes Richard to be a murderer, and he brings accusation against Thomas Mowbray, Duke of Norfolk, partly as a means of embarrassing the King, whom he cannot accuse directly. Mowbray's lot is an unenviable one: he was in command at Calais when Gloucester was executed there, and he hints that Richard ordered the execution (even though Mowbray alleges that he himself did not carry out the order). For his part, Richard is only too glad to banish the man suspected of having been his agent in murder. Mowbray is a convenient scapegoat.

The polished, ceremonial tone of the play's opening is vitiated, then, by our growing awareness of hidden violence and factionalism going on behind the scene. Our first impression of Richard is of a king devoted to the public display of conciliatory even-handedness. He listens to the rival claims of Bolingbroke and Mowbray, and, when he cannot reconcile them peacefully, he orders a trial by combat. This trial (1.3) is replete with ceremonial repetition and ritual. The combatants are duly sworn in the justice of their cause, and God is to decide the quarrel by awarding victory to the champion who speaks the truth. Richard, the presiding officer, assumes the role of God's anointed deputy on earth. Yet it becomes evident in due course that Richard is a major perpetrator of injustice rather than an impartial judge, that Bolingbroke is after greater objectives than he acknowledges even to himself, and that Richard's refusal to let the trial by combat take place and his banishment of the two contenders are his desperate ways of burying a problem he cannot deal with forthrightly. His uncles reluctantly consent to the banishment only because they, too, see that disaffection has reached alarming proportions.

Bolingbroke's motivation in these opening scenes is perhaps even more obscure than Richard's. Our first impression of Bolingbroke is of forthrightness, moral indignation, and patriotic zeal. In fact, we never really question the earnestness of his outrage at Richard's misgovernance, his longing to avenge a family murder (for Gloucester was his uncle, too), or his bitter disappointment at being banished. Yet we are prompted to ask further: what is the essential cause of the enmity between Bolingbroke and Richard? If Mowbray is only a stalking-horse, is not Gloucester's death also the excuse for pursuing a preexistent animosity? Richard, for one, appears to think so. His portrayal of Bolingbroke as a scheming politician, who curries favor with the populace in order to build a widely based alliance against the King himself, is telling and prophetic. Bolingbroke, says Richard, acts "As were our England in reversion his, / And he our subjects' next degree in hope" (1.4.35–6). This unflattering appraisal might be ascribed to malicious envy on Richard's part, were it not proved by subsequent events to be wholly accurate.

Paradoxically, Richard is far the more prescient of the two contenders for the English throne. It is he, in fact, who perceives from the start that the conflict between them is irreconcilable. He banishes Bolingbroke as his chief rival and does not doubt what motives will call Bolingbroke home again. Meanwhile, Bolingbroke disclaims any motive for his return other than love of country and hatred of injustice. Although born with a political canniness that Richard lacks, Bolingbroke does not reflect (out loud, at least) upon the consequences of his own acts. As a man of action, he lives in the present. Richard, conversely, a person of exquisite contemplative powers and poetic imagination, does not deign to cope with the practical. He both envies and despises Bolingbroke's easy way with the commoners. Richard cherishes kingship for the majesty and the royal prerogative it confers, not for the power to govern wisely. Thus it is that, despite his perception of what will follow, Richard habitually indulges his worst instincts, buying a moment of giddy pleasure at the expense of future disaster.

Granted Richard's incompetence as a ruler, is Bolingbroke justified in armed rebellion against him? According to Bolingbroke's uncle, the Duke of York (who later, to be sure, shifts his allegiance), and to the Bishop of Carlisle, Bolingbroke is not justified in the rebellion. The attitude of these men can be summed up by the phrase "passive obedience." And, although Bolingbroke's own father, John of Gaunt, dies before his son returns to England to seize power, Gaunt, too, is opposed to such human defiances of the sacred institution of kingship. "God's is the quarrel," he insists (1.2.37). Because Richard is God's anointed deputy on earth, as Gaunt sees the matter, only God may punish the King's wrongdoing. Gaunt may not question Richard's guilt, but neither does he question God's ability to avenge. Gaunt sees human intervention in God's affair as blasphemous: "for I may never lift / An angry arm against His minister" (1.2.40–1). To be sure, Gaunt does acknowledge a solemn duty to offer frank advice to extremists of both sides, and he does so unsparingly. He consents to the banishment of his son, and he rebukes Richard with his dying breath.

This doctrine of passive obedience was familiar to Elizabethans, for they heard it in church periodically in official homilies against rebellion. It was the Tudor state's answer to those who asserted a right to overthrow reputedly evil kings. The argument was logically ingenious. Why are evil rulers permitted to govern from time to time? Presumably, because God wishes to test a people or to punish them for waywardness. Any king performing such chastisement is a divine scourge. Accordingly, the worst thing a people can do is to rebel against God's scourge, thereby manifesting more waywardness. Instead, they must attempt to remedy the insolence in their hearts, advise the King to mend his ways, and patiently await God's pardon. If they do so, they will not long be disappointed. The doctrine is essentially conservative, defending the status quo. It is reinforced in this play by the Bishop of Carlisle's prophecy that God will avenge through civil war the deposition of his anointed (4.1.126–50); an Elizabethan audience would have appreciated the irony of the prophecy's having come true and having been the subject of Shakespeare's first historical tetralogy. Moreover, in *Richard II* the doctrine of passive obedience is a moderate position between the extremes of tyranny and rebellion, and is expressed by thoughtful, selfless characters. We might be tempted to label it Shakespeare's view if we did not also perceive that the doctrine is continually placed in ironic conflict with harsh political realities. The character who most reflects the ironies and even ludicrous incongruities of the position is the Duke of York.

York is to an extent a choric character, that is, one who helps direct our viewpoint, because his transfer of loyalties from Richard to Bolingbroke structurally delineates the decline of Richard's fortunes and the concurrent rise of Bolingbroke's. At first York shares his brother Gaunt's unwillingness to act, despite their dismay at Richard's willfulness. It is only when Richard seizes the dukedom of Lancaster that York can no longer hold his tongue. His condemnation is as bitter as that of Gaunt, hinting even at loss of allegiance (2.1.200–8). Still, he accepts the responsibility, so cavalierly bestowed by Richard, of governing England in the King's absence. He musters what force he can to oppose Bolingbroke's advance and lectures against this rebellion with the same vehemence he had used against Richard's despotism. Yet, when faced with Bolingbroke's overwhelming military superiority, he accedes rather than fights on behalf of a lost cause. However much this may resemble cowardice or mere expediency, it also displays a pragmatic logic. Once Bolingbroke has become de facto king, in York's view, he must be acknowledged and obeyed. By a kind of analogy to the doctrine of passive obedience (which more rigorous theorists would never allow), York accepts the status quo as inevitable. He is vigorously ready to defend the new regime, just as he earlier defended Richard's de jure rule. York's inconsistent loyalty helps define the structure of the play.

When, however, this conclusion brings York to the point of turning in his own son, Aumerle, for a traitor and quarreling with his wife as to whether their son shall live, the ironic absurdity is apparent. Bolingbroke, now King Henry, himself is amused, in one of the play's rare lighthearted moments (5.3.79–80). At the same time, the comedy deals with serious issues, especially the conflict between public responsibility urged by York and private or emotional satisfaction urged by his Duchess—a conflict seen earlier, for example, in the debate between Gaunt and his sister-in-law, the widowed Duchess of Gloucester (1.2). When a family and a kingdom are divided against one another, there can be no really satisfactory resolution.

We are never entirely convinced that all the fine old medieval theories surrounding kingship—divine right, passive obedience, trial by combat, and the like—can ever wholly explain or remedy the complex and nasty political situation afflicting England. The one man capable of decisive action, in fact, is he who never theorizes at all: Bolingbroke. As we have seen, his avowed motive for opposing Mowbray—simple patriotic indignation—is uttered with such earnestness that we wonder if indeed Bolingbroke has examined those political ambitions in himself that are so plainly visible to Richard and others. This same discrepancy between surface and depth applies to Bolingbroke's motives in returning to England. We cannot be sure at what time he begins to plot that return; the conspiracy announced by Northumberland (2.1.224–300) follows so closely after Richard's violation of Bolingbroke's hereditary rights and is already so well advanced that we gain the impression of an already existing plot, though some of this impression may be simply owing to Shakespeare's characteristic compression of historic time. When Bolingbroke arrives in England, in any case, he protests to York with seemingly passionate sincerity that he comes only for his dukedom of Lancaster (2.3.113–36). If so, why does he set about executing Richard's followers without legal authority and otherwise establishing his own claim to power? Why does he indulge in homophobic slurs against Richard, insinuating that Richard's favorites have "Broke the possession of a royal bed" (3.1.13), when, as far as we can see from the devotion Richard shows to his queen, the charges are trumped up and untrue? Does Bolingbroke seriously think he can reclaim his dukedom by force and then yield to Richard without either maintaining Richard as a puppet king or placing himself in intolerable jeopardy? And can he suppose that his allies, Northumberland and the rest, who have now openly defied the King, will countenance the return to power of one who would never trust them again? It is in this context that York protests, "Well, well, I see the issue of these arms" (2.3.152). The deposition of Richard and then Richard's death are unavoidable conclusions once Bolingbroke has succeeded in an armed rebellion. There can be no turning back. Yet Bolingbroke simply will not think in these terms. He permits Northumberland to proceed with almost sadistic harshness in the arrest and impeachment of Richard and then admonishes Northumberland in public for acting so harshly; the dirty work goes forward, with Northumberland taking the blame, while Bolingbroke assumes a statesmanlike pose. When the new King Henry discovers—to his surprise, evidently—that Richard's life is now a burden to the state, he ponders aloud, "Have I no friend will rid me of this living fear?" (5.4.2) and then rebukes Exton for proceeding on cue.

Bolingbroke's pragmatic spirit and new mode of governing are the embodiment of de facto rule. Ultimately, the justification for his authority is the very fact of its existence, its functioning. Bolingbroke is the man of the hour. To apply William Butler Yeats's striking contrast, the Lancastrian usurpers, Bolingbroke and his son, are vessels of clay, whereas Richard is a vessel of porcelain. One is durable and utilitarian, yet unattractive; the other is exquisite, fragile, and impractical. The comparison does not force us to prefer one to the other, even though Yeats himself characteristically sided with beauty against politics. Rather, Shakespeare gives us our choice, allowing us to see in ourselves an inclination toward political and social stability or toward artistic temperament.

The paradox may suggest that the qualities of a good administrator are not those of a sensitive, thoughtful man. However hopeless as a king, Richard stands before us increasingly as an introspective and fascinating person. The contradictions of his character are aptly focused in the business of breaking a mirror during his deposition: it is at once symbolic of a narcissistic, shallow concern for appearances and a quest for a deeper, inward truth, so that the smashing of the mirror is an act both of self-destruction and of self-discovery. When Richard's power crumbles, his spirit is enhanced, as though loss of power and royal identity were necessary for the discovery of true values.

In this there is a faint anticipation of King Lear's self-learning, fearfully and preciously bought. The trace is only slight here, because in good part Richard II is a political history play rather than a tragedy and because Richard's self-realization is imperfect.

Nevertheless, when Richard faces deposition and separation from his queen, and especially when he is alone in prison expecting to die, he strives to understand his life and through it the general condition of humanity. He gains our sympathy in the wonderfully humane interchange between this deposed king and the poor groom of his stable, who once took care of Richard's horse, roan Barbary, now the possession of the new monarch (5.5.67–94). Richard perceives a contradiction in heaven's assurances about salvation: Christ promises to receive all God's children, and yet He also warns that it is as hard for a rich man to enter heaven as for a camel to be threaded through a needle's eye (5.5.16–17). The paradox echoes the Beatitudes: the last shall be first, the meek shall inherit the earth. Richard, now one of the downtrodden, gropes for an understanding of the vanity of human achievement whereby he can aspire to the victory Christ promised. At his death, that victory seems to him assured: his soul will mount to its seat on high "Whilst my gross flesh sinks downward, here to die" (line 112).

In this triumph of spirit over flesh, the long downward motion of Richard's worldly fortune is crucially reversed. By the same token, the worldly success of Bolingbroke is shown to be no more than that: worldly success. His archetype is Cain, the primal murderer of a brother. To the extent that the play is a history, Bolingbroke's de facto success is a matter of political relevance; but, in the belated movement toward Richard's personal tragedy, we experience a profound countermovement that partly achieves a purgative sense of atonement and reassurance. Whatever Richard may have lost, his gain is also great.

Balance and symmetry are unusually important in *Richard II*. The play begins and ends with elaborate ritual obeisance to the concept of social and monarchic order, and yet, in both cases, a note of personal disorder refuses to be subdued by the public ceremonial. Shakespeare keeps our response to both Richard and Bolingbroke ambivalent by clouding their respective responsibilities for murder. Just as Richard's role in Gloucester's death remains unclear, so Bolingbroke's role in the assassination of Richard remains equally unclear. Mowbray and Exton, as scapegoats, are in some respects parallel. Because Richard and Bolingbroke are both implicated in the deaths of near kinsmen, both are associated with Cain's murder of Abel. As Bolingbroke rises in worldly fortune, Richard falls; as Richard finds insight and release through suffering, Bolingbroke finds guilt and remorse through distasteful political necessity. Verbally and structurally, the play explores the rhetorical figure of chiasmus, or the pairing of opposites in an inverted and diagonal pattern whereby one goes down as the other goes up and vice versa. Again and again, the ritual effects of staging and style draw our attention to the balanced conflicts between the two men and within Richard. Symmetry helps to focus these conflicts in visual and aural ways. In particular, the deposition scene, with its spectacle of a coronation in reverse, brings the sacramental and human sides of the central figure into poignant dramatic relationship.

Women play a subsidiary role in this play about male struggles for power, and yet the brief scenes in which women take part—the Duchess of Gloucester with Gaunt (1.2), Richard's queen with his courtiers and gardeners and then with Richard himself (2.2, 3.4, 5.1), the Duchess of York with her husband and son and King Henry (5.2–5.3)—highlight for us important thematic contrasts between the public and private spheres, power and powerlessness, political struggle and humane sensitivity, the state and the family. The women, excluded from roles of practical authority, offer, nonetheless, an invaluable critical perspective on the fateful and often self-consuming political games that men play among themselves. As in *Julius Caesar* and *Troilus and Cressida*, the men of *Richard II* ignore women's warnings and insights to their own peril and to the discomfiting of the body politic.

The imagery of *Richard II* reinforces structure and meaning. The play is unlike the history plays that follow in its extensive use of blank verse and rhyme and in its interwoven sets of recurring images; *Richard II* is, in this respect, more typical of the so-called lyric period (c. 1594–1596) that also produced *Romeo and Juliet* and *A Midsummer Night's Dream*. Image patterns locate the play in our imaginations as a kind of lost Eden. England is a garden mismanaged by her royal gardener, so that weeds and caterpillars (e.g., Bushy, Bagot, and Green) flourish. The "garden" scene (3.4), located near the center of the play, offering a momentary haven of allegorical reflection on the play's hectic events, is central in the development of the garden metaphor. England is also a sick body, ill-tended by her royal physician, and a family divided against itself, yielding abortive and sterile progeny. Her political ills are attested to by disorders in the cosmos: comets, shooting stars, withered bay trees, and weeping rains. Night owls, associated with death, prevail over the larks of morning. The sun, royally associated at first with Richard, deserts him for Bolingbroke and leaves Richard as the Phaëthon who has mishandled the sun god's chariot and so scorched the earth. Linked to the sun image is the prevalent leitmotif of ascent and descent. And, touching on all these, a cluster of biblical images sees England as a despoiled garden of Eden witnessing a second fall of humanity. Richard repeatedly brands his enemies and deserters as Judases and Pilates—not always fairly; nonetheless, in his last agony, he finds genuine consolation in Christ's example. For a man so self-absorbed in the drama of his existence, this poetic method is intensely suitable. Language and stage action have combined perfectly to express the conflict between a sensitive but flawed king and his efficient but unlovable successor.

RICHARD II

ON STAGE

Richard II was popular with Shakespeare's audience, retaining its appeal well beyond the year of its first performance (probably 1596). The politically ambitious Earl of Essex was "often present at the playing thereof," according to evidence given at the trial of John Hayward in 1600, and it is clear that one reason for the play's continuing presence in the repertory was its political relevance. The fact that Shakespeare's company was commissioned to perform a revival on the eve of Essex's abortive rebellion in 1601 (see the play's Introduction) testifies to the immediacy of the controversy about Richard's unhappy reign and its potential applicability to Elizabethan politics.

Richard II must have been first performed at the Theatre in Shoredich, north of London, and then at the Globe Theatre. The play admirably demonstrates how these theaters, essentially devoid of scenery, featuring a large bare platform with two or more stage doors and a gallery above and to the rear of the stage, could be used to invoke a world of impressive pageantry and political conflict. One key to its staging is the use of symmetry. In the first scene and then again in scene 3, Bolingbroke and Mowbray meet as antagonists from opposite sides of the stage. The elaborate ceremony of trial by combat in scene 3 is conducted in symmetrically antiphonal movements: trumpet signals answer one another, the appellants each enter accompanied by a herald, and the Lord Marshal asks them in turn to state their names and causes, according to prescribed ritual. King Richard, meantime, is enthroned in a raised location, no doubt center stage, symbolically above the level of the combatants.

When it is time to bid them farewell, he literally condescends to them—that is, descends to their level. The canopied and resplendent throne, carried on stage for this scene, provides a commanding stage property. Richard dominates the scene with his theatrical gestures. The whole effect is one of royal magnificence and ceremonial occasion; the playhouse visually embodies, and seems to celebrate, the institution of kingship. Yet it does so ironically in this play, for Richard's royal splendor only masks the prodigality and irresponsibility of his rule.

The encounter of King Richard and Bolingbroke at Flint Castle in act 3, scene 3, uses this same theatrical environment to express in visual terms the taut and delicate negotiations for control taking place between these two contenders. Bolingbroke, illegally back from exile, finds Richard at Flint Castle in Wales and lays siege to that fortress. The presence of the castle is established on the Elizabethan stage not by scenery but by gesture and verbal invocation of "the limits of yon lime and stone" and "the rude ribs of that ancient castle" (ll. 26–32). The Elizabethan theater building needs no scenic assistance to answer this description, for it presents to the spectators an imposing facade with a gallery above, betokening the walls of Flint Castle, and a bare stage representing the ground in front of the castle where the besieging army of Bolingbroke is gathered. Shakespeare's use of the spatial dimensions of this arena seems carefully planned. Bolingbroke resolves on a parley before laying active siege, and so he dispatches his chief supporter, Northumberland, to go with a trumpeter to the walls and demand audience. Bolingbroke and his forces will meantime march "here," "Upon the grassy carpet of this plain"—that is, the front of the stage, which we understand to represent the ground lying at some distance from the castle. Northumberland advances to the castle, a trumpet sounds, and Richard appears *on the walls*—that is, in the gallery above the stage, looking down on those who surround him. Richard should be impressively attired on this momentous occasion (as indeed he was, for example, in Brian Bedford's performance at Stratford, Ontario, in 1983). He icily condemns the affront to his royal authority but knows he can do nothing. Northumberland, trafficking back and forth from King to challenger, proposes in due course the terms of a face-saving surrender: Richard must come down into the "base court" of the castle, to its outer or lower court, where he will receive Bolingbroke's homage. Richard's descent is metaphorical, like the setting of the sun or the fall of Phaëthon to which he alludes, but it is also a literal action in the theater. So is Bolingbroke's kneeling to Richard; it betokens formal obedience, but an obedience that is rendered only after Bolingbroke has obtained the crucial right of his return to England. Once again an impressively ceremonial scene expresses through visual irony the contrast between ritual order and the political reality of conflict and overthrow.

The climactic instance of this kind of inverted or interrupted ceremony in *Richard II* is the trial and deposition of Richard (4.1)—a coronation in reverse. Since no precedents are to be found for such a ritual, Richard invents the form of his own undoing; he commands the scene, though he must lose all. The scene is filled with abortive ritual. Bolingbroke undertakes to mount the throne as King Henry IV but is interrupted by the Bishop of Carlisle; instead, the throne remains vacant for the entire sequence as an eloquent stage symbol of disputed royal authority. Richard offers the crown to Bolingbroke ("Here, cousin, seize the crown") and then holds on to it, refusing to relinquish his last vestige of power without an unseemly struggle, and so the two men grapple unceremoniously for the symbolic object that Bolingbroke had hoped to attain through a more dignified proceeding. At every turn, this play explores visually the tension between ceremony and the realities of power.

On stage in the Restoration and eighteenth century, *Richard II* was regarded chiefly as a political play in which the dilemmas of royal misrule and illegal deposition remained highly controversial. Indeed, as long as English viewers were concerned about the political consequences of the seventeenth-century civil war and subsequent struggles to achieve a balance between monarchy and constitutionalism, *Richard II* seemed as timely as it had for the followers of the Earl of Essex. Dismay at the misgovernance of the Stuart monarchs gave topical significance to Nahum Tate's adaptation in 1680. Fears of renewed rebellion, of forced abdication, and of mob violence were as painfully timely in 1680 as they appeared to have been in Richard II's reign. In spite of Tate's efforts to make the character of Richard personally attractive, the play was banned before it could be performed. By January of 1681, Tate had produced a suggestively titled revision, *The Sicilian Usurper*, sometimes referred to as *The Tyrant of Sicily*, but this, too, attracted the censor's attention with its updated portrayal of an irresponsible royal martyr and was "silenced on the third day" with the Theatre Royal, Drury Lane, itself closed for ten days as punishment. Lewis Theobald took an opposite tack in his adaptation of 1719, making "some innovations upon history and Shakespeare," as he said, in an attempt to blunt any antimonarchical application. His solution was to sentimentalize the story, in part, by adding a love plot between Aumerle and a Lady Piercy newly introduced into the action. John Rich returned to a more critical view of government in his production of *Richard II* at the Theatre Royal, Covent Garden, in 1738, by seeing Shakespeare's play as an indictment of governmental oppression and mismanagement and hence a timely commentary on stage licensing laws recently introduced by Robert Walpole.

Once the issue of monarchical authority had been largely resolved, on the other hand, the emphasis of productions became increasingly sentimental, usually focusing on Richard's tragic role as a sensitively poetic man destroyed by his own political willfulness. Nineteenth-century actors in the grand oratorical style, such as Edmund Kean and Edwin Booth, found the cadences of Richard's speech well suited to tragically moving delivery. Kean produced the play in 1815 in an adaptation by Richard Wroughton that emphasized scenes of high emotion, including an invented one between the Queen and Bolingbroke in which she pleads to be allowed to visit Richard and moves

Bolingbroke with such eloquence that he resolves to return the crown, only to be defeated in his virtuous resolve by Exton's precipitate murder of Richard. The Queen, equally defeated by the swift-moving action, arrives too late to see Richard before he dies.

The nineteenth-century actor-managers also did everything they could through the use of magnificent sets and visual effects to intensify the awe and majesty of Richard's fall and Bolingbroke's rise to power. Charles Kean's spectacular production at the Princess's Theatre in 1857 featured a series of splendid Gothic architectural locations: St. Stephen's chapel, Pembroke Castle, Flint Castle, Milford Harbor, Westminster Hall, the Traitors' Gate of the Tower, the dungeon in Pomfret Castle, and still others. These effects reached their visual climax in the scene of Richard's entry into London in the custody of Bolingbroke—a scene that in Shakespeare's play is described by the Duke of York to his wife (5.2) rather than being staged. Kean not only put the event on stage but added a huge cast of extras: dancing itinerant fools, observers crowding the streets and housetops, and a procession of craft guilds, minstrels, and flower girls. Bolingbroke entered in armor and on horseback; Richard's entrance brought a moment of stunned silence, then murmurs from the mob and increasingly loud calls for vengeance. The visual splendor was devised not only to provide an impressive display but to enhance the pity of Richard's overthrow. Herbert Beerbohm Tree, in one of his most opulently mounted historical revivals (at His Majesty's Theatre, 1903), managed to outdo Kean. Not only did Tree's Richard and Bolingbroke, like Kean's, enter on horseback in act 5, scene 2, but also Mowbray and Bolingbroke rode into the lists at Coventry in act 1, scene 3; and Tree provided other spectacular effects, including a lavish coronation scene for Bolingbroke to contrast with the pathos of Richard's solitude and victimization.

Such opulence and scenic inflexibility could not continue indefinitely. Encouraged by the example of William Poel and his efforts with the Elizabethan Stage Society (1899, with a then

unknown amateur named Harley Granville-Barker as Richard)
to recover the pacing and nonillusionistic staging practices of
Shakespeare's theater, twentieth-century directors have generally brought an end to cumbersome sets and operatic grand emo-
tions, eschewing Victorian sentimentality to explore the deeper
psychological roots of an action generally conceived as Richard's
tragedy. Harcourt Williams, at London's Old Vic in 1929, strove
for a fast-paced, naturalistic performance that would, he said, do
away with "the absurd convention of the Shakespearean voice."
As portrayed by John Gielgud, the Richard of Williams's production failed politically because of his excessive self-pity and
his willingness to retreat into fantasy. Gielgud returned to the
part in 1937 at the Queen's Theatre, himself directing a production that emphasized Richard's self-indulgent extravagance.
Gielgud once again directed the play, in 1952 at the Lyric
Theatre, Hammersmith, this time with Paul Scofield as a tragically isolated Richard. At New York's St. James Theater in 1937,
Margaret Webster's production starred Maurice Evans as a flighty
and frivolous king who turns away from the world and into himself as his political fortunes decline. Ralph Richardson directed
the play in 1947 at London's New Theatre, with Alec Guinness
in the title role as "a proud weakling" who, in J. C. Trewin's
phrase, "uses irony as a defense." In 1951 Michael Redgrave
starred in Anthony Quayle's production at Stratford-upon-Avon
as a sensitive and self-absorbed Richard, infatuated with failure,
ill-suited to the political world into which he was born.

Other productions have been more attuned to a skeptical
vision of the world of political struggle, ironically bringing the
stage history of Richard II full circle, returning to it the political
focus, though one less narrowly topical, that determined much
of its early popularity. In 1964, at Stratford-upon-Avon, Peter
Hall, John Barton, and Clifford Williams directed Richard II
and both parts of Henry IV in an extended dramatic exploration
of the triumph of realpolitik. David Warner's peremptory and
petulant Richard was no match for Eric Porter's purposefully
Machiavellian Bolingbroke. John Barton's version of 1973 at

Stratford-upon-Avon used the devices of the modern theater to call attention to the means by which theatrical illusion is made, thereby suggesting the illusions that politics depends upon and even the illusory character of life itself. Bolingbroke and Mowbray in the lists at Coventry were mounted on hobbyhorses, in order to underscore the hollow nature of the ritual. The figure of Death was repeatedly present: in the Duchess of Gloucester's last scene on earth (1.2), in the garden scene when the gardeners were habited as monks (3.4), and as the presiding figure in the final scene. The groom visiting Richard in prison turned out to be Bolingbroke in disguise. Richard's coffin in act 5, scene 6, was only large enough for a child. Richard Pasco and Ian Richardson alternated as Richard and Bolingbroke in different performances to stress a sense of interchangeability in the protagonists. However different from one another in style and character, the capricious king and his usurping cousin were seen as finally alike in their vulnerability to the ironies of history, both of them playing games of state without fully comprehending or controlling their destinies.

More recent productions have similarly acknowledged the grim necessity of history itself. Terry Hands, at Stratford-upon-Avon in 1980, directed Alan Howard as an energetic and intelligent Richard, one who improvised strategies of survival while realizing nonetheless that he must inevitably fall before the quiet strength of David Suchet's pragmatic Bolingbroke. Howard movingly shifted from the feverish arrogance of the early scenes to a contemplative and ironic vision of a world he no longer could or even wished to control. Hands's production, like Barton's, showed the play's power on the stage to articulate a vision of history shockingly modern in its disillusioned sense of the political process. Bolingbroke inherited a throne that could no longer be propped up with the traditional myths of authority, and the mourning of the final scene was as much for England's troubled future as for Richard's tragic past. Ron Daniels's production for the RSC in Stratford-upon-Avon, which opened in November 1990 (and moved to London's Barbican Theatre the following fall), was arguably even more gloomy. Black was the color dominating the stage and costumes, broken only by Richard's blood-red throne and his red and blue velvet robe. Alex Jennings's Richard was decidedly unsympathetic, exploiting the sharp contrast between the actor's elegant carriage and the guilty wariness of his looks. In opposition was Anton Lesser's Bolingbroke, a man decidedly unenthusiastic about the crown that seemed to stalk him; it was indeed for "Lancaster" that he returned, and he backed away in fear when Richard handed the crown to him. In Daniels's production, one saw neither Henry's Machiavellian political abilities nor Richard's sensitive, poetic spirit: one was offered a consistent, coherent, but always discouraging vision of a world that found its dominant image in the huge steel curtain dividing the stage, which inevitably recalled the late twentieth century's images of inhuman tyranny.

Other productions have moved away from an exclusive focus on the dispiriting politics to explore the fascinating emotional issues that play presents. Joseph Papp, in his 1987 production for the New York Shakespeare Festival in the Delacorte Theater, Central Park, saw the play as a conflict between a Richard (Peter MacNicol) who was sometimes bored with the affairs of state and his intimidating rival Bolingbroke (John Bedford Lloyd). MacNicol's Richard was sensitive, complex, funny at times, born to be a martyr, a fiasco as a ruler but ennobled by his ruin. Papp strove for a quintessentially "American" *Richard II*, one that did not take the play too seriously or echo the solemnities of Gielgud's influential tragic interpretation (as seen also in Jeremy Irons's portrayal of Richard in Barry Kyle's production at Stratford-upon-Avon in 1986). Yet Papp's resistance to what had become almost cliché in late twentieth-century productions was finally less remarkable than the production at London's Royal National Theatre at the Cottesloe, which opened in June 1995. Deborah Warner, among the most inventive of British directors, cast Fiona Shaw as Richard. Critics were uncertain whether this was a brilliant stroke or a gimmick, but Shaw proved an extraordinary Richard. Her own interests were not political. "I was not interested in the Richard who was king," she said in an interview. Instead she explored the relationship between Richard and Bolingbroke, cousins who inhabit the same world, who love, rather than hate, each other, but must strive to destroy the other, even with that knowledge. Reinforced by an uncanny physical resemblance between Shaw and David Threefall, who played Bolingbroke, the production took its energy from the deep connection between them. They shared a language, both verbal and gestural, that marked them as long-time admirers of each other, each subconsciously adopting the style of the other. It was a production not always successful but one that opened up areas of the play often ignored, not least the comedy in the role, a self-conscious clowning that Richard used to voice and manage his awareness of the ironies of the political situation he had in fact created for himself.

In spring of 2000, the RSC, at the Other Place in Stratford-upon-Avon, mounted a production of the play, imaginatively directed by Steven Pimlott, that found its center in the relationship of the action with the audience, which was made to feel complicit with the political events (unlike the almost simultaneous production directed by Jonathan Kent and starring Ralph Fiennes at London's Almeida Theatre, which, probably unsurprisingly, was a star turn, with Fiennes's Richard genuinely believing in the divine right of kings). Seated on simple metal bleachers, and not in darkness, the audience at the Other Place was lit by the stage lights as it faced an almost bare, whitewashed stage. It was regularly engaged by the characters, who were always aware that success in this political world demands the support of the commoners who are watching. At one point, the audience was sharply ordered to stand in silence following the announcement of Mowbray's death—and dutifully they did so. The play, in its exploration of power and performance, effectively exploited the contrasts between Sam West's slight, boyish Richard and David Traughton's imposing, experienced Bolingbroke, yet what differences one saw in style were erased at the end, as Henry echoed Richard's soliloquy studying how he might compare his prison to the world while Henry now took up the crown, all too aware of the course to which he has committed himself. Pimlott's production suggested what *Richard II* can be on stage by avoiding the too-easy denigration of politics and attending to the sharp emotional edges of Shakespeare's text; in productions like this one we can see the timeless pertinence of this historical drama that Shakespeare's first audiences immediately saw as a comment on the politics of their own generation.

RICHARD II
ON SCREEN

Shakespeare could not, of course, have imagined a world in which people would see performances of his plays projected onto large or small screens rather than acted live in theaters, but that has become the case. In the more than one hundred years since the first film of a Shakespeare play was made (in 1899, an excerpt from Sir Herbert Beerbohm Tree's production of *King John*), the screen has become Shakespeare's proper medium no less than the stage or the printed page. If Shakespeare's works are undisputedly literary classics and staples of our theatrical repertories, they have also inescapably become a part of the modern age's love affair with film. In a movie theater, on a television screen, or on a DVD player, Shakespeare's plays live for us, and thereby reach audiences much greater than those that fill our theaters.

It is, however, a development not always welcomed. Some critics complain that Shakespeare on screen is different from (and worse than) Shakespeare in the theater. Certainly it is a distinct experience to see a play in a darkened movie theater with actors larger than life. It is different, too, to see it on a television screen with actors smaller than they are in life, and where the experience of play watching is inevitably more private than in any theater.

But there are obvious advantages as well. On screen, performances are preserved and allowed easily to circulate. If films of Shakespeare may sometimes lack the exhilarating provisionality of live theater, they gain the not insignificant benefit of easy accessibility. In a town without a theater company one can see a Shakespeare play virtually at will. Some newly filmed version of a Shakespeare play is seemingly released every year. A video or DVD can be rented even if the film itself has passed from the local cineplex. And on video we can replay—even interrupt—the performance, allowing it to repeat itself as we attend to details that might otherwise be missed.

Filmed Shakespeare is indeed different from staged Shakespeare or Shakespeare read, but it is no less valuable for being so. It provides a way—and for most of us the most convenient way—to see the plays. For people who cannot get to the theater and who find the printed text difficult to imagine as a theatrical experience, filmed Shakespeare offers easy access to a performance. For students for whom the language of a play often seems (and indeed is) stilted and archaic, the enactment clarifies the psychological and social relations of the characters. For all of us who love Shakespeare, his availability on film gives us an archive of performances to be viewed and enjoyed again and again. It is no less an authentic experience than seeing Shakespeare in the theater, for the modern theater (even the self-conscious anachronisms like the rebuilt Globe) imposes its own anachronisms upon the plays (as indeed does a modern printed edition like this one). And arguably, as many like to claim, if Shakespeare lived today he would most likely have left Stratford for Hollywood.

Although *Richard II* has yet to be made into a feature-length film, it has been televised several times. In fact, it was the first of Shakespeare's English history plays to be made into a full-length television production, by the BBC in 1950. In 1954, NBC followed suit with a lavish *Hallmark Hall of Fame* program, broadcast live in fifty-five U.S. cities. It starred Maurice Evans in what was widely regarded as his best Shakespearean role, along with Sarah Churchill as Richard's queen, Kent Smith as Bolingbroke, and Morton Da Costa as Aumerle.

For its Age of Kings series in 1960, the BBC mounted a production, based on acts 1 through 3 of *Richard II*, that won for director Peter Dews and director Michael Hayes the British Guild of Directors' award for excellence in directing. David William played the King, opposite Tom Fleming as Bolingbroke. A young Sean Connery took the role of Hotspur—a minor part in this play, but fully developed in *1 Henry IV.* Since the Age of Kings presented its fifteen episodes in chronological order rather than in the order that Shakespeare had written them, this selected portion of *Richard II* had the honor of leading off the series.

In 1978 as well, the BBC chose to lead off its ambitiously comprehensive new project, the Shakespeare Plays, with *Richard II.* With Derek Jacobi as King Richard, John Gielgud as Gaunt, Jon Finch as Bolingbroke, and Wendy Hiller as the Duchess of York, this is a memorable production, clearly one of the best of the series (along with *Hamlet,* also starring Derek Jacobi). Its rhetorical high points, including John of Gaunt's deathbed litany of loving praise for "this sceptered isle" and of dire warning to his prodigal young nephew-king (2.1), and Richard's somber reflections comparing "this prison where I live unto the world" (5.5), elevate Shakespeare's language to the high level of performance art that it merits. Some reviewers have seen the production as confirming the cliché that *Richard II* is better poetry than drama, but at least it is great poetry.

A Bard Production of *Richard II,* released in 1982 in the United States, with David Birney as the King, takes place on a bare stage. American actors pay respectful attention to Shakespeare's language without feeling the constraint of adopting British accents or styles of delivery.

Richard II
Filmography

1. 1950
   BBC
   Royston Morley and Graeme Muir, producers
   Royston Morley, director

   King Richard II—Alan Wheatley
   Henry Bolingbroke—Clement McCallin
   John of Gaunt—Henry Oscar

2. 1954
   NBC/Hallmark
   Maurice Evans and Albert McCleery, producers
   George Schaefer, director

   King Richard II—Maurice Evans
   Henry Bolingbroke—Kent Smith
   John of Gaunt—Fredric Worlock

3. 1960—*The Hollow Crown* and *The Deposing of a King*
   (*An Age of Kings*, episodes 1 and 2)
   BBC
   Peter Dews, producer
   Michael Hayes, director

   King Richard II—David William
   Henry Bolingbroke—Tom Fleming
   John of Gaunt—Edgar Wreford
   Duke of York—Geoffrey Bayldon
   Northumberland—George A. Cooper
   Queen—Juliet Cooke
   Hotspur—Sean Connery

4. 1970
   BBC/Prospect Theatre Company
   Mark Shivas, producer
   Richard Cottrell and Toby Robertson, directors

   King Richard II—Ian McKellen
   Henry Bolingbroke—Timothy West
   John of Gaunt—Paul Hardwick
   Queen—Lucy Fleming

5. 1978
   BBC/Time-Life Television
   Cedric Messina, producer
   David Giles, director

King Richard II—Derek Jacobi
Henry Bolingbroke—Jon Finch
John of Gaunt—John Gielgud
Duke of York—Charles Gray
Queen—Janet Maw
Duchess of York—Wendy Hiller

6. 1982
   Bard Productions
   Jack Nakano and Jack Manning, producers
   William Woodman, director

   King Richard II—David Birney
   Henry Bolingbroke—Paul Shenar
   John of Gaunt—John McLiam
   Duke of York—Peter MacLean
   Queen—Mary Joan Negro

7. 1991—*The Wars of the Roses: Richard II*
   BBC/English Shakespeare Company
   John Paul Chapple and Andy Ward, producers
   Michael Bogdanov, director

   King Richard II—Michael Pennington
   Henry Bolingbroke—Michael Cronin
   John of Gaunt—Clyde Pollit
   Duke of York—Colin Farrell
   Queen—Francesca Ryan
   Hotspur—Andrew Jarvis

8. 1997
   BBC/Royal National Theatre
   Shaun Deeny and John Wyver, producers
   Deborah Warner, director

King Richard II—Fiona Shaw
Henry Bolingbroke—Richard Brenner
John of Gaunt—Graham Crowden

9. 2003
BBC/The Globe Theatre
Tim Carroll, director

King Richard II—Mark Rylance
Henry Bolingbroke—Liam Brennan
John of Gaunt—John McEnery
Queen—Michael Brown

THE PLAYHOUSE

From other contemporary evidence, including the stage directions and dialogue of Elizabethan plays, we can surmise that the various public theaters where Shakespeare's plays were produced (the Theatre, the Curtain, the Globe) resembled the Swan in many important particulars, though there must have been some variations as well. The public playhouses were essentially round, or polygonal, and open to the sky, forming an acting arena approximately 70 feet in diameter; they did not have a large curtain with which to open and close a scene, such as we see today in opera and some traditional theater. A platform measuring approximately 43 feet across and 27 feet deep, referred to in the de Witt drawing as the *proscaenium*, projected into the yard, *planities sive arena*. The roof, *tectum*, above the stage and supported by two pillars, could contain machinery for ascents and descents, as were required in several of Shakespeare's late plays. Above this roof was a hut, shown in the drawing with a flag flying atop it and a trumpeter at its door announcing the performance of a play. The underside of the stage roof, called the heavens, was usually richly decorated with symbolic figures of the sun, the moon, and the constellations. The platform stage stood at a height of 5½ feet or so above the yard, providing room under the stage for underworldly effects. A trapdoor, which is not visible in this drawing, gave access to the space below.

The structure at the back of the platform (labeled *mimorum aedes*), known as the tiring-house because it was the actors' attiring (dressing) space, featured at least two doors, as shown here. Some theaters seem to have also had a discovery space, or curtained recessed alcove, perhaps between the two doors—in which Falstaff could have hidden from the sheriff (*1 Henry IV*, 2.4) or Polonius could have eavesdropped on Hamlet and

~

*This early copy of a drawing by Johannes de Witt of the Swan
Theatre in London (c. 1596), made by his friend Arend van
Buchell, is the only surviving contemporary sketch of the interior
of a public theater in the 1590s.*

his mother (*Hamlet*, 3.4). This discovery space probably gave the actors a means of access to and from the tiring-house. Curtains may also have been hung in front of the stage doors on occasion. The de Witt drawing shows a gallery above the doors that extends across the back and evidently contains spectators. On occasions when action "above" demanded the use of this space, as when Juliet appears at her "window" (*Romeo and Juliet*, 2.2 and 3.5), the gallery seems to have been used by the actors, but large scenes there were impractical.

The three-tiered auditorium is perhaps best described by Thomas Platter, a visitor to London in 1599 who saw on that occasion Shakespeare's *Julius Caesar* performed at the Globe:

> The playhouses are so constructed that they play on a raised platform, so that everyone has a good view. There are different galleries and places [*orchestra, sedilia, porticus*], however, where the seating is better and more comfortable and therefore more expensive. For whoever cares to stand below only pays one English penny, but if he wishes to sit, he enters by another door [*ingressus*] and pays another penny, while if he desires to sit in the most comfortable seats, which are cushioned, where he not only sees everything well but can also be seen, then he pays yet another English penny at another door. And during the performance food and drink are carried round the audience, so that for what one cares to pay one may also have refreshment.

Scenery was not used, though the theater building itself was handsome enough to invoke a feeling of order and hierarchy that lent itself to the splendor and pageantry on stage. Portable properties, such as thrones, stools, tables, and beds, could be carried or thrust on as needed. In the scene pictured here by de Witt, a lady on a bench, attended perhaps by her waiting-gentlewoman, receives the address of a male figure. If Shakespeare had written *Twelfth Night* by 1596 for performance at the Swan, we could imagine Malvolio appearing like this as he bows before the Countess Olivia and her gentlewoman, Maria.

RICHARD II

~ஃ~

KING RICHARD THE SECOND

QUEEN, *Richard's wife*

JOHN OF GAUNT, *Duke of Lancaster, King Richard's uncle*

HENRY BOLINGBROKE, *John of Gaunt's son, Duke of
    Hereford and claimant to his father's dukedom
    of Lancaster, later King Henry IV*

DUKE OF YORK, *Edmund of Langley, King Richard's uncle*

DUCHESS OF YORK

DUKE OF AUMERLE, *York's son and the Earl of Rutland*

DUCHESS OF GLOUCESTER, *widow of Thomas of Woodstock,
    Duke of Gloucester (King Richard's uncle)*

THOMAS MOWBRAY, *Duke of Norfolk,*

EARL OF SALISBURY,

LORD BERKELEY,

DUKE OF SURREY,

BISHOP OF CARLISLE,

SIR STEPHEN SCROOP,

ABBOT OF WESTMINSTER,

BUSHY,

BAGOT, } *favorites of King Richard,*

GREEN,

CAPTAIN *of the Welsh Army,*

*supporters of King
Richard*

EARL OF NORTHUMBERLAND,
HARRY PERCY, *Northumberland's son,*
LORD ROSS,
LORD WILLOUGHBY,
LORD FITZWATER,
SIR PIERCE OF EXTON,
Another LORD,

supporters of Bolingbroke

LORD MARSHAL
Two HERALDS
GARDENER
GARDENER'S MAN
LADY *attending the Queen*
KEEPER *of the prison*
A MAN *attending Exton*

SERVINGMAN *to York*
GROOM *of the stable*

Lords, Officers, Soldiers, Attendants,
  Ladies attending the Queen

SCENE: *England and Wales*]

1.1 *Location: A room of state.* (Holinshed's *Chronicles* places this scene at Windsor, in 1398.)

1 **Old John of Gaunt** (Born in 1340 at Ghent; hence the surname *Gaunt*. In 1398 he was fifty-eight years old.)

4 **late** recent.   **appeal** accusation, formal challenge or impeachment that the accuser was obliged to maintain in combat

5 **our, us** (The royal plural.)   **leisure** i.e., lack of leisure

7 **liege** i.e., sovereign.

8 **sounded** inquired of

9 **appeal** accuse.   **on . . . malice** on the grounds of long-standing enmity

12 **sift** discover by questioning.   **argument** subject

13 **apparent** obvious, manifest

16 **ourselves** I myself. (The royal plural.)

18 **High-stomached** Haughty 傲慢

[1.1] ❧ *Enter King Richard, John of Gaunt, with other*
nobles and attendants.

KING RICHARD
Old John of Gaunt, time-honored Lancaster,   1
Hast thou according to thy oath and bond
Brought hither Henry Hereford, thy bold son,
Here to make good the boist'rous late appeal,   4
Which then our leisure would not let us hear,   5
Against the Duke of Norfolk, Thomas Mowbray?

GAUNT   I have, my liege.   7

KING RICHARD
Tell me, moreover, hast thou sounded him   8
If he appeal the Duke on ancient malice,   9
Or worthily, as a good subject should,
On some known ground of treachery in him?

GAUNT
As near as I could sift him on that argument,   12
On some apparent danger seen in him   13
Aimed at Your Highness, no inveterate malice.

KING RICHARD
Then call them to our presence.   [*Exit an attendant.*]
                                   Face to face,
And frowning brow to brow, ourselves will hear   16
The accuser and the accusèd freely speak.
High-stomached are they both, and full of ire;   18
In rage, deaf as the sea, hasty as fire.

        Enter Bolingbroke and Mowbray.

22 **Each . . . happiness** May each day improve on the happiness of other past days

23 **hap** fortune

26 **you come** for which you come

28 **what . . . object** what accusation do you bring

30 **record** witness

32 **Tend'ring** watching over, holding dear

34 **appellant** as the accuser

38 **answer** answer for

39 **miscreant** irreligious villain

40 **good** i.e., noble, high-born

41 **crystal** clear. (The image alludes to the crystal spheres in which, according to the Ptolemaic conception of the universe, the heavenly bodies were fixed.)

43 **aggravate the note** emphasize the stigma, i.e., the charge of treason

45 **so please** if it please

46 **right-drawn** justly drawn

47 **accuse my zeal** cast doubt on my zeal or loyalty.

48 **woman's war** i.e., war of words

49 **eager** sharp, biting

BOLINGBROKE
> Many years of happy days befall
> My gracious sovereign, my most loving liege!

MOWBRAY
> Each day still better others' happiness,   22
> Until the heavens, envying earth's good hap,   23
> Add an immortal title to your crown!

KING RICHARD
> We thank you both. Yet one but flatters us,
> As well appeareth by the cause you come: 26
> Namely, to appeal each other of high treason.
> Cousin of Hereford, what dost thou object   28
> Against the Duke of Norfolk, Thomas Mowbray?

BOLINGBROKE
> First—heaven be the record to my speech!—   30
> In the devotion of a subject's love,
> Tend'ring the precious safety of my prince,   32
> And free from other misbegotten hate,
> Come I appellant to this princely presence.   34
> Now, Thomas Mowbray, do I turn to thee;
> And mark my greeting well, for what I speak
> My body shall make good upon this earth
> Or my divine soul answer it in heaven.   38
> Thou art a traitor and a miscreant.   39
> Too good to be so and too bad to live,   40
> Since the more fair and crystal is the sky,   41
> The uglier seem the clouds that in it fly.
> Once more, the more to aggravate the note,   43
> With a foul traitor's name stuff I thy throat,
> And wish, so please my sovereign, ere I move,   45
> What my tongue speaks my right-drawn sword may prove.   46

MOWBRAY
> Let not my cold words here accuse my zeal.   47
> 'Tis not the trial of a woman's war,   48
> The bitter clamor of two eager tongues,   49

50 **Can** that can

56 **post** ride at high speed (like a messenger riding relays of horses)

58 **Setting . . . royalty** Disregarding Bolingbroke's royal blood (as grandson of Edward III)

59 **let him be** suppose him to be

63 **tied** obliged

65 **inhabitable** uninhabitable

69 **gage** a pledge to combat (usually a glove or gauntlet, i.e., a mailed or armored glove)

70 **Disclaiming** relinquishing.   **kindred** kinship

72 **except** exempt, set aside.

74 **pawn** i.e., the gage

77 **or . . . devise** or anything worse you can imagine to have been said about you.

Can arbitrate this cause betwixt us twain;   50
The blood is hot that must be cooled for this.
Yet can I not of such tame patience boast
As to be hushed and naught at all to say.
First, the fair reverence of Your Highness curbs me
From giving reins and spurs to my free speech,
Which else would post until it had returned   56
These terms of treason doubled down his throat.
Setting aside his high blood's royalty,   58
And let him be no kinsman to my liege,   59
I do defy him, and I spit at him,
Call him a slanderous coward and a villain;
Which to maintain I would allow him odds
And meet him, were I tied to run afoot   63
Even to the frozen ridges of the Alps
Or any other ground inhabitable   65
Wherever Englishman durst set his foot.
Meantime, let this defend my loyalty:
By all my hopes, most falsely doth he lie.

BOLINGBROKE [*throwing down his gage*]
I   Pale trembling coward, there I throw my gage,   69
Disclaiming here the kindred of the King,   70
And lay aside my high blood's royalty,
Which fear, not reverence, makes thee to except.   72
If guilty dread have left thee so much strength
As to take up mine honor's pawn, then stoop.   74
By that, and all the rites of knighthood else,
Will I make good against thee, arm to arm,
What I have spoke or thou canst worse devise.   77

MOWBRAY [*taking up the gage*]
I take it up; and by that sword I swear
Which gently laid my knighthood on my shoulder,
I'll answer thee in any fair degree
Or chivalrous design of knightly trial;

82 **light** alight, dismount

85 **inherit us** put me in possession of, make me have

87 **Look what** Whatever

88 **nobles** gold coins worth six shillings eight pence

89 **lendings** advances on pay

90 **lewd** vile, base

93 **Or** either

95 **these eighteen years** i.e., ever since the Peasants' Revolt of 1381

96 **Complotted** plotted in a conspiracy

97 **Fetch** derive. **head and spring** (Synonymous words meaning "origin.")

100 **Duke of Gloucester's death** (Thomas of Woodstock, Duke of Gloucester, a younger son of Edward III and brother of John of Gaunt, was murdered at Calais in September 1397, while in Mowbray's custody.)

101 **Suggest . . . adversaries** did prompt Gloucester's easily persuaded enemies (to believe him guilty of treason)

102 **consequently** afterward

103 **Sluiced out** let flow (as by the opening of a sluice, or valve)

104 **Abel's** (For the story of Cain's murder of his brother Abel, the first such murder on earth and the archetype of the killing of a kinsman, see Genesis 4:3–12.)

105 **tongueless** resonant but without articulate speech; echoing

109 **pitch** highest reach of a falcon's flight

And when I mount, alive may I not light   82
If I be traitor or unjustly fight!

KING RICHARD
What doth our cousin lay to Mowbray's charge?
It must be great that can inherit us   85
So much as of a thought of ill in him.

BOLINGBROKE
Look what I speak, my life shall prove it true: 87
That Mowbray hath received eight thousand nobles   88
In name of lendings for Your Highness' soldiers,   89
The which he hath detained for lewd employments,   90
Like a false traitor and injurious villain.
Besides I say, and will in battle prove
Or here or elsewhere to the furthest verge   93
That ever was surveyed by English eye,
That all the treasons for these eighteen years   95
Complotted and contrivèd in this land   96
Fetch from false Mowbray their first head and
    spring.   97
Further I say, and further will maintain
Upon his bad life to make all this good,
That he did plot the Duke of Gloucester's death,   100
Suggest his soon-believing adversaries,   101
And consequently, like a traitor coward,   102
Sluiced out his innocent soul through streams of
    blood—   103
Which blood, like sacrificing Abel's, cries   104
Even from the tongueless caverns of the earth   105
To me for justice and rough chastisement.
And, by the glorious worth of my descent,
This arm shall do it or this life be spent.

KING RICHARD
How high a pitch his resolution soars!   109
Thomas of Norfolk, what say'st thou to this?

113 **this slander . . . blood** this disgrace to the royal
family

118 **my scepter's awe** the reverence due my scepter

120 **nothing** not at all.   **partialize** make partial, bias

126 **receipt** money received

129 **For that** because

130 **Upon . . . account** for the balance of a heavy debt

131 **Since . . . queen** (Mowbray went in 1395 to France to
negotiate the King's marriage to Isabella, daughter of
the French King Charles VI, but Richard himself es-
corted her to England.)

132–4 **For . . . case** (Mowbray speaks guardedly but seems
to imply that he postponed the execution of Gloucester that he was ordered by Richard to carry out.)

132 **For** As for

140 **exactly** (1) explicitly (2) fully

142 **appealed** of which I am charged

MOWBRAY

Oh, let my sovereign turn away his face
And bid his ears a little while be deaf,
Till I have told this slander of his blood 113
How God and good men hate so foul a liar!

KING RICHARD

Mowbray, impartial are our eyes and ears.
Were he my brother, nay, my kingdom's heir,
As he is but my father's brother's son,
Now, by my scepter's awe I make a vow, 118
Such neighbor nearness to our sacred blood
Should nothing privilege him nor partialize 120
The unstooping firmness of my upright soul.
He is our subject, Mowbray; so art thou.
Free speech and fearless I to thee allow.

MOWBRAY

Then, Bolingbroke, as low as to thy heart
Through the false passage of thy throat thou liest!
Three parts of that receipt I had for Calais 126
Disbursed I duly to His Highness' soldiers;
The other part reserved I by consent,
For that my sovereign liege was in my debt 129
Upon remainder of a dear account 130
Since last I went to France to fetch his queen. 131
Now swallow down that lie. For Gloucester's death, 132
I slew him not, but to my own disgrace 133
Neglected my sworn duty in that case. 134
[*To Gaunt*] For you, my noble lord of Lancaster,
The honorable father to my foe,
Once did I lay an ambush for your life,
A trespass that doth vex my grievèd soul;
But ere I last received the Sacrament
I did confess it, and exactly begged 140
Your Grace's pardon, and I hope I had it.
This is my fault. As for the rest appealed, 142

144 **recreant** cowardly; or, coward (used as a noun)

145 **Which** which charge.   **in myself** in my own person

146 **interchangeably** in exchange, reciprocally

147 **overweening** arrogant, proud

149 **Even in** by shedding

150 **In haste whereof** To hasten which proof of my innocence

153 **Let's . . . blood** let's treat this wrath (caused by an excess of bile or choler) by purging (vomiting or evacuation) rather than by medical bloodletting. (With a play on "bloodshed in combat.")

156 **conclude** come to a final agreement

157 **no month to bleed** (Learned authorities often differed as to which months or seasons were best for medicinal bloodletting.)

164 **boot** help for it.

165 **Myself I throw** i.e., I throw myself, instead of my gage

168 **Despite . . . grave** that will live in the epitaph on my grave in spite of devouring Death

It issues from the rancor of a villain,
A recreant and most degenerate traitor,   144
Which in myself I boldly will defend,   145
And interchangeably hurl down my gage   146
Upon this overweening traitor's foot,   147
To prove myself a loyal gentleman
Even in the best blood chambered in his bosom.   149

[*He throws down his gage. Bolingbroke picks it up.*]

In haste whereof most heartily I pray   150
Your Highness to assign our trial day.

KING RICHARD
Wrath-kindled gentlemen, be ruled by me;
Let's purge this choler without letting blood.   153
This we prescribe, though no physician;
Deep malice makes too deep incision.
Forget, forgive; conclude and be agreed;   156
Our doctors say this is no month to bleed.—   157
Good uncle, let this end where it begun;
We'll calm the Duke of Norfolk, you your son.

GAUNT
To be a make-peace shall become my age.
Throw down, my son, the Duke of Norfolk's gage.

KING RICHARD
And Norfolk, throw down his.

GAUNT   When, Harry, when?
Obedience bids I should not bid again.

KING RICHARD
Norfolk, throw down, we bid; there is no boot.   164

MOWBRAY [*kneeling*]
Myself I throw, dread sovereign, at thy foot.   165
My life thou shalt command, but not my shame.
The one my duty owes; but my fair name,
Despite of death that lives upon my grave,   168
To dark dishonor's use thou shalt not have.

170 **impeached** accused.   **baffled** publicly dishonored

173 **Which . . . poison** of him who uttered this slander.

174 **Lions . . . tame** (The royal arms showed a lion rampant; Mowbray's emblem was a leopard.)

175 **spots** (1) leopard spots (2) stains of dishonor.

177 **mortal times** our earthly lives

182 **in one** inseparably

184 **try** put to the test

186 **throw . . . gage** i.e., surrender your gage up to me, thereby ending the quarrel. (Richard is probably seated on a raised throne, as in scene 3.)

189 **impeach my height** discredit my high rank

190 **out-dared** dared down, cowed.   **dastard** coward.

191 **feeble wrong** dishonorable submission

192 **sound . . . parle** trumpet so shameful a negotiation, i.e., consent to ask a truce

192–5 **my teeth . . . face** my teeth will bite off my tongue as a craven instrument of cowardly capitulation and spit it out bleeding, to its (the tongue's) great disgrace, into Mowbray's face, where shame abides perpetually.

195.1 *Exit Gaunt* (A stage direction from the Folio, adopted by most editors so that Gaunt will not be required to exit at the end of scene 1 and then immediately reenter.)

I am disgraced, impeached, and baffled here,   170
Pierced to the soul with slander's venomed spear,
The which no balm can cure but his heart-blood
Which breathed this poison.

KING RICHARD   Rage must be withstood.   173
Give me his gage. Lions make leopards tame.   174

MOWBRAY
Yea, but not change his spots. Take but my shame,   175
And I resign my gage. My dear dear lord,
The purest treasure mortal times afford   177
Is spotless reputation; that away,
Men are but gilded loam or painted clay.
A jewel in a ten-times-barred-up chest
Is a bold spirit in a loyal breast.
Mine honor is my life; both grow in one;   182
Take honor from me, and my life is done.
Then, dear my liege, mine honor let me try;   184
In that I live, and for that will I die.

KING RICHARD [to Bolingbroke]
Cousin, throw up your gage; do you begin.   186

BOLINGBROKE
Oh, God defend my soul from such deep sin!
Shall I seem crestfallen in my father's sight?
Or with pale beggar-fear impeach my height   189
Before this out-dared dastard? Ere my tongue   190
Shall wound my honor with such feeble wrong,   191
Or sound so base a parle, my teeth shall tear   192
The slavish motive of recanting fear   193
And spit it bleeding in his high disgrace,   194
Where shame doth harbor, even in Mowbray's face.   195

                                            [Exit Gaunt.]

KING RICHARD
We were not born to sue but to command;
Which since we cannot do to make you friends,
Be ready, as your lives shall answer it,

199 **Saint Lambert's day** September 17.

202 **atone** reconcile

203 **design . . . chivalry** designate who is the true chivalric victor.

205 **home alarms** domestic conflicts.

1.2 *Location: John of Gaunt's house.* **(? No place is speci-fied, and the scene is not in Holinshed.)**

1 **the part . . . blood** my kinship with Thomas of Wood-stock, the Duke of Gloucester (i.e., as my older brother)

2 **exclaims** exclamations

3 **stir** take action

4 **those hands** i.e., Richard's (whom Gaunt charges with responsibility for Gloucester's death)

11 **Edward's** Edward III's

21 **envy's** malice's

At Coventry upon Saint Lambert's day.   199
There shall your swords and lances arbitrate
The swelling difference of your settled hate.
Since we cannot atone you, we shall see   202
Justice design the victor's chivalry.   203
Lord Marshal, command our officers at arms
Be ready to direct these home alarms.   205

                                        Exeunt.

[1.2] ❧ *Enter John of Gaunt with the Duchess of*
            Gloucester.

GAUNT

Alas, the part I had in Woodstock's blood   1
Doth more solicit me than your exclaims   2
To stir against the butchers of his life!   3
But since correction lieth in those hands   4
Which made the fault that we cannot correct,
Put we our quarrel to the will of heaven,
Who, when they see the hours ripe on earth,
Will rain hot vengeance on offenders' heads.

DUCHESS

Finds brotherhood in thee no sharper spur?
Hath love in thy old blood no living fire?
Edward's seven sons, whereof thyself art one,   11
Were as seven vials of his sacred blood
Or seven fair branches springing from one root.
Some of those seven are dried by nature's course,
Some of those branches by the Destinies cut;
But Thomas, my dear lord, my life, my Gloucester,
One vial full of Edward's sacred blood,
One flourishing branch of his most royal root,
Is cracked, and all the precious liquor spilt,
Is hacked down, and his summer leaves all faded,
By envy's hand and murder's bloody ax.   21

23 **metal** substance out of which a person or a thing is made. (With a sense too of *mettle,* "temperament, disposition.")   **self** selfsame

25 **consent** acquiesce

28 **model** likeness, copy

31 **naked** i.e., undefended

33 **mean** lowly

37 **God's substitute** i.e., the King, God's deputy on earth

39 **his** i.e., Gloucester's

42 **complain myself** lodge a complaint on my own behalf.

46 **cousin** kinsman.   **fell** fierce

47 **sit . . . wrongs** may my husband's wrongs sit

49 **misfortune** i.e., Mowbray's downfall.   **career** charge of the horse in a tourney or combat

Ah, Gaunt, his blood was thine! That bed, that womb,
That metal, that self mold that fashioned thee,   23
Made him a man; and though thou livest and
    breathest,
Yet art thou slain in him. Thou dost consent   25
In some large measure to thy father's death
In that thou see'st thy wretched brother die,
Who was the model of thy father's life.   28
Call it not patience, Gaunt; it is despair.
In suff'ring thus thy brother to be slaughtered,
Thou showest the naked pathway to thy life,   31
Teaching stern murder how to butcher thee.
That which in mean men we entitle patience   33
Is pale cold cowardice in noble breasts.
What shall I say? To safeguard thine own life
The best way is to venge my Gloucester's death.

GAUNT
God's is the quarrel; for God's substitute,   37
His deputy anointed in His sight,
Hath caused his death; the which if wrongfully   39
Let heaven revenge, for I may never lift
An angry arm against His minister.

DUCHESS
Where then, alas, may I complain myself?   42

GAUNT
To God, the widow's champion and defense.

DUCHESS
Why, then, I will. Farewell, old Gaunt.
Thou goest to Coventry, there to behold
Our cousin Hereford and fell Mowbray fight.   46
Oh, sit my husband's wrongs on Hereford's spear,   47
That it may enter butcher Mowbray's breast!
Or if misfortune miss the first career,   49
Be Mowbray's sins so heavy in his bosom
That they may break his foaming courser's back

52 **lists** barriers enclosing the tournament area

53 **caitiff** base, cowardly

54 **sometimes** late

58 **boundeth** bounces, rebounds, returns. (The Duchess apologizes for speaking yet again; her grief, she says, continues on and on, like a bouncing tennis ball.)

59 **Not . . . weight** (Grief is not hollow, like a tennis ball, but continues to move because of its heaviness.)

60 **begun** i.e., begun to grieve

62 **Edmund York** Edmund of Langley, fifth son of Edward III.

66 **Pleshey** Gloucester's country seat, in Essex

68 **unfurnished** bare

69 **offices** service quarters, workrooms

1.3 *Location: The lists at Coventry. Scaffolds or raised seats are provided for the King and his nobles, and chairs are provided for the combatants.*

  2 **at all points** completely.   **in** i.e., into the lists, the space designed for combat.

And throw the rider headlong in the lists,   52
A caitiff recreant to my cousin Hereford!   53
Farewell, old Gaunt. Thy sometimes brother's wife   54
With her companion, Grief, must end her life.

GAUNT
Sister, farewell. I must to Coventry.
As much good stay with thee as go with me!

DUCHESS
Yet one word more. Grief boundeth where it falls,   58
Not with the empty hollowness, but weight.   59
I take my leave before I have begun,   60
For sorrow ends not when it seemeth done.
Commend me to thy brother, Edmund York.   62
Lo, this is all. Nay, yet depart not so!
Though this be all, do not so quickly go;
I shall remember more. Bid him—ah, what?—
With all good speed at Pleshey visit me.   66
Alack, and what shall good old York there see
But empty lodgings and unfurnished walls,   68
Unpeopled offices, untrodden stones,   69
And what hear there for welcome but my groans?
Therefore commend me; let him not come there
To seek out sorrow that dwells everywhere.
Desolate, desolate, will I hence and die.
The last leave of thee takes my weeping eye.   *Exeunt.*

[1.3] ❧ *Enter Lord Marshal and the Duke [of] Aumerle.*

MARSHAL
My Lord Aumerle, is Harry Hereford armed?

AUMERLE
Yea, at all points, and longs to enter in.   2

3 **sprightfully** with high spirit
4 **Stays** awaits
9 **orderly** according to the rules
13 **quarrel** complaint.
18 **defend** forbid
21 **appeals** accuses

MARSHAL
 The Duke of Norfolk, sprightfully and bold,   3
 Stays but the summons of the appellant's trumpet. 4

AUMERLE
 Why then the champions are prepared, and stay
 For nothing but His Majesty's approach.

> *The trumpets sound, and the King enters with his*
> *nobles [Gaunt, Bushy, Bagot, Green, and others].*
> *When they are set, enter [Mowbray] the Duke of*
> *Norfolk in arms, defendant, [with a herald].*

KING RICHARD
 Marshal, demand of yonder champion
 The cause of his arrival here in arms.
 Ask him his name, and orderly proceed   9
 To swear him in the justice of his cause.

MARSHAL [*to Mowbray*]
 In God's name and the King's, say who thou art
 And why thou comest thus knightly clad in arms,
 Against what man thou com'st, and what thy quarrel. 13
 Speak truly on thy knighthood and thy oath,
 As so defend thee heaven and thy valor!

MOWBRAY
 My name is Thomas Mowbray, Duke of Norfolk,
 Who hither come engagèd by my oath—
 Which God defend a knight should violate!— 18
 Both to defend my loyalty and truth
 To God, my king, and my succeeding issue
 Against the Duke of Hereford that appeals me, 21
 And by the grace of God and this mine arm
 To prove him, in defending of myself,
 A traitor to my God, my king, and me;
 And as I truly fight, defend me heaven!

28 **plated** armored.   **habiliments** the attire

30 **Depose him** take his sworn deposition

43 **daring-hardy** daringly bold, reckless.   **touch** i.e., interfere in

47 **bow my knee** (Presumably Bolingbroke kneels to Richard and, at about line 69, to Gaunt.)

51 **several** various

The trumpets sound. Enter [Bolingbroke,] Duke of
Hereford, appellant, in armor, [with a herald].

KING RICHARD

    Marshal, ask yonder knight in arms

    Both who he is and why he cometh hither

    Thus plated in habiliments of war;   28

    And formally, according to our law,

    Depose him in the justice of his cause.   30

MARSHAL *[to Bolingbroke]*

    What is thy name? And wherefore com'st thou
        hither,

    Before King Richard in his royal lists?

    Against whom comest thou? And what's thy quarrel?

    Speak like a true knight, so defend thee heaven!

BOLINGBROKE

    Harry of Hereford, Lancaster, and Derby

    Am I, who ready here do stand in arms

    To prove, by God's grace and my body's valor,

    In lists, on Thomas Mowbray, Duke of Norfolk,

    That he is a traitor foul and dangerous

    To God of heaven, King Richard, and to me;

    And as I truly fight, defend me heaven!

MARSHAL

    On pain of death, no person be so bold

    Or daring-hardy as to touch the lists,   43

    Except the Marshal and such officers

    Appointed to direct these fair designs.

BOLINGBROKE

    Lord Marshal, let me kiss my sovereign's hand

    And bow my knee before His Majesty;   47

    For Mowbray and myself are like two men

    That vow a long and weary pilgrimage.

    Then let us take a ceremonious leave

    And loving farewell of our several friends.   51

55 **as** insofar as

56 **royal fight** i.e., a fight taking place in the presence of the King.

59–60 **profane . . . For me** misuse tears by weeping for me

66 **lusty** full of vigor.   **cheerly** cheerfully

67 **regreet** greet, salute

68 **The daintiest** i.e., the most tasty, the finest. (Bolingbroke refers to the custom of ending banquets with a sweet dessert.)

70 **regenerate** born anew

71 **twofold** i.e., of father and son

73 **proof** invulnerability

75 **enter . . . coat** pierce Mowbray's armor as though it were made of wax

76 **furbish** polish

77 **lusty havior** vigorous behavior, deportment

81 **amazing** bewildering.   **casque** helmet

MARSHAL [to King Richard]
    The appellant in all duty greets Your Highness
    And craves to kiss your hand and take his leave.

KING RICHARD [coming down]
    We will descend and fold him in our arms.

                          [He embraces Bolingbroke.]

    Cousin of Hereford, as thy cause is right,   55
    So be thy fortune in this royal fight!   56
    Farewell, my blood—which if today thou shed,
    Lament we may, but not revenge thee dead.

BOLINGBROKE
    Oh, let no noble eye profane a tear   59
    For me if I be gored with Mowbray's spear.   60
    As confident as is the falcon's flight
    Against a bird do I with Mowbray fight.
    [To the King] My loving lord, I take my leave of you;
    [To Aumerle] Of you, my noble cousin, Lord Aumerle;
    Not sick, although I have to do with death,
    But lusty, young, and cheerly drawing breath.   66
    Lo, as at English feasts, so I regreet   67
    The daintiest last, to make the end most sweet.   68
    [To Gaunt] O thou, the earthly author of my blood,
    Whose youthful spirit, in me regenerate,   70
    Doth with a twofold vigor lift me up   71
    To reach at victory above my head,
    Add proof unto mine armor with thy prayers,   73
    And with thy blessings steel my lance's point
    That it may enter Mowbray's waxen coat   75
    And furbish new the name of John o' Gaunt   76
    Even in the lusty havior of his son.   77

GAUNT
    God in thy good cause make thee prosperous!
    Be swift like lightning in the execution,
    And let thy blows, doubly redoubled,
    Fall like amazing thunder on the casque   81

84 **Mine . . . thrive!** May my innocence and the protectorship of Saint George bring me victory!

90 **enfranchisement** freedom

94 **Take . . . years** take from me the wish that you may enjoy many happy years.

95 **gentle** unperturbed in spirit.   **to jest** i.e., to a play or entertainment

96 **quiet** calm

97 **Securely** Confidently

98 **couchèd** lodged, expressed, leveled in readiness (as with a lance)

102 **Strong . . . hope** (Alludes to Psalm 61:3: "for thou hast been my hope, and a strong tower for me against the face of the enemy.")

Of thy adverse pernicious enemy.
Rouse up thy youthful blood, be valiant, and live.

BOLINGBROKE
Mine innocence and Saint George to thrive! 84

MOWBRAY
However God or fortune cast my lot,
There lives or dies, true to King Richard's throne,
A loyal, just, and upright gentleman.
Never did captive with a freer heart
Cast off his chains of bondage and embrace
His golden uncontrolled enfranchisement 90
More than my dancing soul doth celebrate
This feast of battle with mine adversary.
Most mighty liege, and my companion peers,
Take from my mouth the wish of happy years. 94
As gentle and as jocund as to jest 95
Go I to fight. Truth hath a quiet breast. 96

KING RICHARD
Farewell, my lord. Securely I espy 97
Virtue with valor couchèd in thine eye.— 98
Order the trial, Marshal, and begin.

MARSHAL
Harry of Hereford, Lancaster, and Derby,
Receive thy lance; and God defend the right!

[A lance is given to Bolingbroke.]

BOLINGBROKE
Strong as a tower in hope, I cry "Amen!" 102

MARSHAL [to an officer]
Go bear this lance to Thomas, Duke of Norfolk.

[A lance is given to Mowbray.]

FIRST HERALD
Harry of Hereford, Lancaster, and Derby
Stands here for God, his sovereign, and himself,

108 **him** himself, Bolingbroke. (See line 40.)

112 **approve** prove

114 **him** i.e., Mowbray. (See line 24.)

116 **Attending** awaiting

118 **warder** staff or truncheon borne by the King when presiding over a trial by combat

122 **While we return** until I inform

122.1 *flourish* fanfare.

124 **list** hear

125 **For that** In order that

127 **for** because (also in line 129)

131 **envy** enmity.   **set on you** set you on

On pain to be found false and recreant,
To prove the Duke of Norfolk, Thomas Mowbray,
A traitor to his God, his king, and him,   108
And dares him to set forward to the fight.

SECOND HERALD
Here standeth Thomas Mowbray, Duke of Norfolk,
On pain to be found false and recreant,
Both to defend himself and to approve   112
Henry of Hereford, Lancaster, and Derby,
To God, his sovereign, and to him disloyal,   114
Courageously and with a free desire
Attending but the signal to begin.   116

MARSHAL
Sound, trumpets, and set forward, combatants!

> [*A charge is sounded. Richard throws
> down his baton.*]

Stay! The King hath thrown his warder down.   118

KING RICHARD
Let them lay by their helmets and their spears,
And both return back to their chairs again.
[*To his counselors*] Withdraw with us, and let the trumpets
    sound
While we return these dukes what we decree.   122

> [*A long flourish. Richard consults apart with
> Gaunt and others.*]

Draw near,
And list what with our council we have done.   124
For that our kingdom's earth should not be soiled   125
With that dear blood which it hath fosterèd;
And for our eyes do hate the dire aspect   127
Of civil wounds plowed up with neighbors' sword;
And for we think the eagle-wingèd pride
Of sky-aspiring and ambitious thoughts,
With rival-hating envy, set on you   131
To wake our peace, which in our country's cradle

134 **Which** i.e., which enmity, disturbance of the peace. (Although, in literal terms, the antecedent of *Which* is *peace* in line 132.)

140 **life** i.e., loss of life

143 **stranger** alien

150 **sly** stealthy.   **determinate** put to an end

151 **dateless limit** unlimited term.   **dear** grievous

156 **dearer merit** better reward.   **maim** injury

162 **viol** a six-stringed instrument, related to the modern violin, played with a curved bow

163 **cunning** skillfully made

164 **open** taken from its case.   **his** that person's

Draws the sweet infant breath of gentle sleep,
Which, so roused up with boist'rous untuned drums,   134
With harsh-resounding trumpets' dreadful bray
And grating shock of wrathful iron arms,
Might from our quiet confines fright fair peace
And make us wade even in our kindred's blood:
Therefore we banish you our territories.
You, cousin Hereford, upon pain of life,   140
Till twice five summers have enriched our fields,
Shall not regreet our fair dominions,
But tread the stranger paths of banishment.   143

BOLINGBROKE
Your will be done. This must my comfort be:
That sun that warms you here shall shine on me,
And those his golden beams to you here lent
Shall point on me and gild my banishment.

KING RICHARD
Norfolk, for thee remains a heavier doom,
Which I with some unwillingness pronounce:
The sly slow hours shall not determinate   150
The dateless limit of thy dear exile.   151
The hopeless word of "never to return"
Breathe I against thee, upon pain of life.

MOWBRAY
A heavy sentence, my most sovereign liege,
And all unlooked-for from Your Highness' mouth.
A dearer merit, not so deep a maim   156
As to be cast forth in the common air,
Have I deservèd at Your Highness' hands.
The language I have learned these forty years,
My native English, now I must forgo;
And now my tongue's use is to me no more
Than an unstringèd viol or a harp,   162
Or like a cunning instrument cased up,   163
Or, being open, put into his hands   164

167 **portcullised** shut in by a portcullis, an iron grating over a gateway that can be raised and lowered

173 **breathing . . . breath** speaking English.

174 **boots** avails.   **compassionate** full of laments.

175 **plaining** complaining

181 **Our part therein** i.e., the duty you owe me as King

187 **louring** threatening, scowling

188 **advisèd** deliberate, premeditated

189 **complot** plot together

That knows no touch to tune the harmony.
Within my mouth you have enjailed my tongue,
Doubly portcullised with my teeth and lips,   167
And dull unfeeling barren ignorance
Is made my jailer to attend on me.
I am too old to fawn upon a nurse,
Too far in years to be a pupil now.
What is thy sentence then but speechless death,
Which robs my tongue from breathing native breath?   173

KING RICHARD
    It boots thee not to be compassionate.   174
    After our sentence plaining comes too late.   175

MOWBRAY
    Then thus I turn me from my country's light,
    To dwell in solemn shades of endless night.

                  [He starts to leave.]

KING RICHARD
    Return again, and take an oath with thee.
    Lay on our royal sword your banished hands.

       [They place their hands on Richard's sword.]

    Swear by the duty that you owe to God—
    Our part therein we banish with yourselves—   181
    To keep the oath that we administer:
    You never shall, so help you truth and God,
    Embrace each other's love in banishment,
    Nor never look upon each other's face,
    Nor never write, regreet, nor reconcile
    This louring tempest of your homebred hate;   187
    Nor never by advisèd purpose meet   188
    To plot, contrive, or complot any ill   189
    'Gainst us, our state, our subjects, or our land.

BOLINGBROKE   I swear.

MOWBRAY   And I, to keep all this.

193 **so far** let me say this much

196 **sepulchre of our flesh** i.e., body, the temple or tomb of the soul

200 **clogging** (A clog was a wooden block attached to the leg to hinder movement.)

206 **stray** take the wrong road

208 **glasses** mirrors (here glistening with tears)

214 **wanton** luxuriant

221 **oil-dried** empty of oil

BOLINGBROKE

Norfolk, so far as to mine enemy: 193
By this time, had the King permitted us,
One of our souls had wandered in the air,
Banished this frail sepulchre of our flesh,   196
As now our flesh is banished from this land.
Confess thy treasons ere thou fly the realm.
Since thou hast far to go, bear not along
The clogging burden of a guilty soul.   200

MOWBRAY

No, Bolingbroke. If ever I were traitor,
My name be blotted from the book of life,
And I from heaven banished as from hence!
But what thou art, God, thou, and I do know,
And all too soon, I fear, the King shall rue.—
Farewell, my liege. Now no way can I stray;   206
Save back to England, all the world's my way.   *Exit.*

KING RICHARD [*to Gaunt*]

Uncle, even in the glasses of thine eyes   208
I see thy grievèd heart. Thy sad aspect
Hath from the number of his banished years
Plucked four away. [*To Bolingbroke*] Six frozen winters
    spent,
Return with welcome home from banishment.

BOLINGBROKE

How long a time lies in one little word!
Four lagging winters and four wanton springs   214
End in a word; such is the breath of kings.

GAUNT

I thank my liege that in regard of me
He shortens four years of my son's exile.
But little vantage shall I reap thereby;
For, ere the six years that he hath to spend
Can change their moons and bring their times about,
My oil-dried lamp and time-bewasted light   221

223 **taper** candle

224 **blindfold Death** i.e., *blindfold* because *Death* deprives
its victims of their sight and because it is often pictured
as an eyeless skull

230 **in his pilgrimage** brought about in time's journey

231 **current** i.e., as good as current coin, valid

232 **dead** i.e., once I am dead.   **buy** i.e., restore with a
payment

234 **a party verdict** one person's share in a joint verdict

240 **smooth** extenuate

241 **partial slander** accusation of partiality (on behalf of
my son)

243 **looked when** expected that, awaited the point at
which

244 **to . . . away** in making away with my own (son)

Shall be extinct with age and endless night;
My inch of taper will be burnt and done,   223
And blindfold Death not let me see my son.   224

KING RICHARD
Why, uncle, thou hast many years to live.

GAUNT
But not a minute, King, that thou canst give.
Shorten my days thou canst with sullen sorrow,
And pluck nights from me, but not lend a morrow;
Thou canst help Time to furrow me with age,
But stop no wrinkle in his pilgrimage;   230
Thy word is current with him for my death,   231
But dead, thy kingdom cannot buy my breath.   232

KING RICHARD
Thy son is banished upon good advice,
Whereto thy tongue a party verdict gave.   234
Why at our justice seem'st thou then to lour?

GAUNT
Things sweet to taste prove in digestion sour.
You urged me as a judge, but I had rather
You would have bid me argue like a father.
Oh, had it been a stranger, not my child,
To smooth his fault I should have been more mild.   240
A partial slander sought I to avoid   241
And in the sentence my own life destroyed.
Alas, I looked when some of you should say   243
I was too strict, to make mine own away;   244
But you gave leave to my unwilling tongue
Against my will to do myself this wrong.

KING RICHARD
Cousin, farewell; and, uncle, bid him so.
Six years we banish him, and he shall go.
                    [*Flourish. Exit King Richard with his train.*]

249 **What . . . know** What I cannot learn from you in person

250 **s.d.** *Exit* (The exit is uncertain; see 1.4.1–4.)

251 **no leave take** I i.e., I will not take my leave of you, my lord; I will not say good-bye

256 **office** function.   **prodigal** lavish

257 **To breathe** in uttering

258 **grief** grievance

259 **grief** unhappiness

262 **travel** (The quarto spelling, "trauaile," suggests an interchangeable meaning of "travel" and "labor.")

265 **sullen** (1) melancholy (2) dull

266 **foil** thin metal leaf set behind gems to show off their luster; hence, that which sets something off to advantage

AUMERLE [*to Bolingbroke*]

    Cousin, farewell. What presence must not know,   249

    From where you do remain let paper show.   [*Exit.*]   250

MARSHAL [*to Bolingbroke*]

    My lord, no leave take I, for I will ride,   251

    As far as land will let me, by your side.

                [*Bolingbroke makes no answer. The Lord Marshal*
                                 stands aside.]

GAUNT [*to Bolingbroke*]

    Oh, to what purpose dost thou hoard thy words,

    That thou returnest no greeting to thy friends?

BOLINGBROKE

    I have too few to take my leave of you,

    When the tongue's office should be prodigal   256

    To breathe the abundant dolor of the heart.   257

GAUNT

    Thy grief is but thy absence for a time.   258

BOLINGBROKE

    Joy absent, grief is present for that time.   259

GAUNT

    What is six winters? They are quickly gone.

BOLINGBROKE

    To men in joy; but grief makes one hour ten.

GAUNT

    Call it a travel that thou tak'st for pleasure.   262

BOLINGBROKE

    My heart will sigh when I miscall it so,

    Which finds it an enforcèd pilgrimage.

GAUNT

    The sullen passage of thy weary steps   265

    Esteem as foil wherein thou art to set   266

    The precious jewel of thy home return.

269 **remember** remind.   **a deal of world** a great distance

272 **passages** wanderings, experiences

273 **Having my freedom** (1) having completed my ap-
prenticeship (2) having been allowed to return home

274 **journeyman** (Literally, one who labors for day wages
as a fully qualified craftsman—with a hint also of one
who makes a journey. Bolingbroke will be proficient
only in grief.)

275 **the eye of heaven** the sun

280 **But . . . King** i.e., but suppose that you are banishing
the King to the moral wilderness his crimes deserve.

280–1 **Woe . . . borne** Woe is all the more oppressive when
it perceives that the sufferer is fainthearted.

282 **purchase** acquire, win

286 **Look what** Whatever

289 **the presence strewed** the royal presence chamber
strewn with rushes

291 **measure** stately, formal dance

292 **gnarling** snarling, growling

293 **sets it light** regards it lightly.

295 **Caucasus** mountain range between the Black and
Caspian seas.

299 **fantastic** imagined

BOLINGBROKE

    Nay, rather every tedious stride I make

    Will but remember me what a deal of world   269

    I wander from the jewels that I love.

    Must I not serve a long apprenticehood

    To foreign passages, and in the end,   272

    Having my freedom, boast of nothing else   273

    But that I was a journeyman to grief?   274

GAUNT

    All places that the eye of heaven visits   275

    Are to a wise man ports and happy havens.

    Teach thy necessity to reason thus:

    There is no virtue like necessity.

    Think not the King did banish thee,

    But thou the King. Woe doth the heavier sit   280

    Where it perceives it is but faintly borne.   281

    Go, say I sent thee forth to purchase honor,   282

    And not the King exiled thee; or suppose

    Devouring pestilence hangs in our air

    And thou art flying to a fresher clime.

    Look what thy soul holds dear, imagine it   286

    To lie that way thou goest, not whence thou com'st.

    Suppose the singing birds musicians,

    The grass whereon thou tread'st the presence strewed,   289

    The flowers fair ladies, and thy steps no more

    Than a delightful measure or a dance;   291

    For gnarling sorrow hath less power to bite   292

    The man that mocks at it and sets it light.   293

BOLINGBROKE

    Oh, who can hold a fire in his hand

    By thinking on the frosty Caucasus?   295

    Or cloy the hungry edge of appetite

    By bare imagination of a feast?

    Or wallow naked in December snow

    By thinking on fantastic summer's heat?   299

302 **Fell** Fierce.   **rankle** cause irritation and festering

303 **lanceth not** does not open the wound (to permit the release of the infection; Bolingbroke's point is that sorrow should be openly confronted, not rationalized or covered over and thus allowed to fester)

304 **bring** escort

305 **stay** linger, stay behind.

1.4 *Location: The court.*

1 **We did observe** (The scene begins in the midst of a conversation.)

4 **next** nearest

6 **for me** on my part.   **except** except that

8 **rheum** watery discharge (i.e., tears)

9 **hollow** insincere

Oh, no, the apprehension of the good
Gives but the greater feeling to the worse.
Fell Sorrow's tooth doth never rankle more   302
Than when he bites but lanceth not the sore.   303

GAUNT
Come, come, my son, I'll bring thee on thy way.   304
Had I thy youth and cause, I would not stay.   305

BOLINGBROKE
Then, England's ground, farewell. Sweet soil, adieu,
My mother and my nurse that bears me yet!
Where'er I wander, boast of this I can:
Though banished, yet a trueborn Englishman.

Exeunt.

[1.4] ❧ *Enter the King, with Bagot, [Green,] etc. at one
door, and the Lord Aumerle at another.*

KING RICHARD
We did observe.—Cousin Aumerle,   1
How far brought you high Hereford on his way?

AUMERLE
I brought high Hereford, if you call him so,
But to the next highway, and there I left him.   4

KING RICHARD
And say, what store of parting tears were shed?

AUMERLE
Faith, none for me, except the northeast wind,   6
Which then blew bitterly against our faces,
Awaked the sleeping rheum and so by chance   8
Did grace our hollow parting with a tear.   9

KING RICHARD
What said our cousin when you parted with him?

12 **for** because

13 **that** i.e., my disdain. (Aumerle says he pretended to be overcome by grief in order to avoid saying an insincere "Farewell" to Bolingbroke.)

16 **Marry** Indeed. (From the oath, "by the Virgin Mary.")

19 **of** from

22 **friends** kinsmen, i.e., us, his cousins.

29 **underbearing** bearing, endurance

30 **banish . . . him** take their affections with him into banishment.

32 **brace of draymen** pair of cart drivers

35 **As . . . his** i.e., as if my England were to revert to him as true owner after my death

36 **our . . . hope** i.e., the heir presumptive to the throne and favorite choice of the people.

37 **go** let go

38 **for** as for.   **stand out** hold out, resist

39 **Expedient manage** speedy arrangements

AUMERLE   "Farewell!"
    And, for my heart disdainèd that my tongue   12
    Should so profane the word, that taught me craft   13
    To counterfeit oppression of such grief
    That words seemed buried in my sorrow's grave.
    Marry, would the word "farewell" have lengthened
       hours   16
    And added years to his short banishment,
    He should have had a volume of farewells;
    But since it would not, he had none of me.   19

KING RICHARD
    He is our cousin, cousin; but 'tis doubt,
    When time shall call him home from banishment,
    Whether our kinsman come to see his friends.   22
    Ourself and Bushy, Bagot here, and Green
    Observed his courtship to the common people,
    How he did seem to dive into their hearts
    With humble and familiar courtesy,
    What reverence he did throw away on slaves,
    Wooing poor craftsmen with the craft of smiles
    And patient underbearing of his fortune,   29
    As 'twere to banish their affects with him.   30
    Off goes his bonnet to an oyster wench;
    A brace of draymen bid God speed him well   32
    And had the tribute of his supple knee,
    With "Thanks, my countrymen, my loving friends,"
    As were our England in reversion his,   35
    And he our subjects' next degree in hope.   36

GREEN
    Well, he is gone, and with him go these thoughts.   37
    Now for the rebels which stand out in Ireland,   38
    Expedient manage must be made, my liege,   39
    Ere further leisure yield them further means
    For their advantage and Your Highness' loss.

43 **for** because.   **too great a court** i.e., too great an extravagance at court

44 **liberal largess** extravagant generosity (to courtiers)

45 **farm** lease the right of collecting taxes, for a present cash payment, to the highest bidder

48 **substitutes** deputies.   **blank charters** writs authorizing the collection of revenues or forced loans to the crown, blank spaces being left for the names of the parties and the sums they were to provide

50 **subscribe them** put down their names

51 **them** i.e., the sums collected

52 **presently** at once.

58 **Ely House** (Palace of the Bishop of Ely in Holborn, a London district.)

61 **lining** contents. (With pun on lining for coats.)   **coats** coats of mail, armor

KING RICHARD
    We will ourself in person to this war.
    And, for our coffers with too great a court   43
    And liberal largess are grown somewhat light,   44
    We are enforced to farm our royal realm,   45
    The revenue whereof shall furnish us
    For our affairs in hand. If that come short,
    Our substitutes at home shall have blank charters, 48
    Whereto, when they shall know what men are rich,
    They shall subscribe them for large sums of gold   50
    And send them after to supply our wants;   51
    For we will make for Ireland presently.   52

       Enter Bushy.

    Bushy, what news?

BUSHY
    Old John of Gaunt is grievous sick, my lord,
    Suddenly taken, and hath sent posthaste
    To entreat Your Majesty to visit him.

KING RICHARD   Where lies he?

BUSHY   At Ely House.   58

KING RICHARD
    Now put it, God, in the physician's mind
    To help him to his grave immediately!
    The lining of his coffers shall make coats   61
    To deck our soldiers for these Irish wars.
    Come, gentlemen, let's all go visit him.
    Pray God we may make haste and come too late!

ALL   Amen.   *Exeunt.*

2.1 *Location: Ely House.*

0.1 *Enter John of Gaunt sick* (Presumably he is carried in by servants in a chair.)

2 **unstaid** uncontrolled

3 **strive . . . breath** i.e., don't waste your breath

8 **they** those persons

9 **He . . . listened more** He who will soon be silenced by death is listened to more

10 **glose** flatter, deceive in speech.

11 **marked** noticed

13 **is sweetest last** is longest remembered as sweet

14 **Writ in remembrance** written down in the memory

15 **my life's counsel** my advice while I lived

16 **My . . . tale** my grave dying speech

18 **As . . . fond** such as praises, which even wise men are foolishly inclined to hear

19 **meters** verses.   **venom** poisonous

21 **proud Italy** (Roger Ascham, John Lyly, and other sixteenth-century writers complained of the growing influence of Italian luxury.)

22 **still** always.   **tardy-apish** imitative but behind the times

❧ *Enter John of Gaunt sick, with the Duke of York,*
        etc.

GAUNT

 Will the King come, that I may breathe my last
 In wholesome counsel to his unstaid youth?   2

YORK

 Vex not yourself, nor strive not with your breath,   3
 For all in vain comes counsel to his ear.

GAUNT

 Oh, but they say the tongues of dying men
 Enforce attention like deep harmony.
 Where words are scarce, they are seldom spent in vain,
 For they breathe truth that breathe their words in pain.   8
 He that no more must say is listened more   9
     Than they whom youth and ease have taught to glose.   10
 More are men's ends marked than their lives before.   11
     The setting sun, and music at the close,
 As the last taste of sweets, is sweetest last,   13
 Writ in remembrance more than things long past.   14
 Though Richard my life's counsel would not hear,   15
 My death's sad tale may yet undeaf his ear.   16

YORK

 No, it is stopped with other, flattering sounds,
 As praises, of whose taste the wise are fond;   18
 Lascivious meters, to whose venom sound   19
 The open ear of youth doth always listen;
 Report of fashions in proud Italy,   21
 Whose manners still our tardy-apish nation   22
 Limps after in base imitation.
 Where doth the world thrust forth a vanity—

25 **So** so long as.   **there's no respect** it makes no difference

28 **Where . . . regard** where natural inclination rebels
against what reason esteems.

29 **Direct . . . choose** Don't try to offer advice to one who
insists on going his own way.

33 **riot** profligacy

36 **betimes** soon, early

38 **Light vanity** frivolous dissipation.   **cormorant** glut-
ton. (Literally, a voracious seabird.)

39 **means** i.e., means of sustenance

41 **earth of majesty** land fit for kings.   **seat of Mars**
residence of the god of war

44 **infection** (1) plague (2) moral pollution

45 **happy breed** fortunate race

47 **office** function

51 **teeming** fruitful

52 **by their breed** for their ancestral reputation for
prowess

55 **stubborn Jewry** i.e., Judea, called stubborn because it
resisted Christianity

So it be new, there's no respect how vile—   25
That is not quickly buzzed into his ears?
Then all too late comes counsel to be heard
Where will doth mutiny with wit's regard.   28
Direct not him whose way himself will choose.   29
'Tis breath thou lack'st, and that breath wilt thou
    lose.

GAUNT
Methinks I am a prophet new inspired,
And thus expiring do foretell of him:
His rash fierce blaze of riot cannot last,   33
For violent fires soon burn out themselves;
Small showers last long, but sudden storms are short;
He tires betimes that spurs too fast betimes;   36
With eager feeding food doth choke the feeder;
Light vanity, insatiate cormorant,   38
Consuming means, soon preys upon itself.   39
This royal throne of kings, this sceptered isle,
This earth of majesty, this seat of Mars,   41
This other Eden, demi-paradise,
This fortress built by Nature for herself
Against infection and the hand of war,   44
This happy breed of men, this little world,   45
This precious stone set in the silver sea,
Which serves it in the office of a wall   47
Or as a moat defensive to a house,
Against the envy of less happier lands,
This blessed plot, this earth, this realm, this England,
This nurse, this teeming womb of royal kings,   51
Feared by their breed and famous by their birth,   52
Renownèd for their deeds as far from home
For Christian service and true chivalry
As is the sepulcher in stubborn Jewry   55
Of the world's ransom, blessèd Mary's son,
This land of such dear souls, this dear dear land,

60 **tenement** land or property held by a tenant.   **pelting**
    paltry

61 **bound in** bordered, surrounded

63 **bound in** legally constrained

64 **blots . . . bonds** i.e., the blank charters.

68 **ensuing** approaching

73 **composition** constitution.

76 **meat** food

77 **watched** kept watch at night, been vigilant

80 **Is . . . fast** is something I must forgo

81 **therein fasting** i.e., since I am starved of that pleasure

83 **inherits** possesses, will receive

Dear for her reputation through the world,
Is now leased out—I die pronouncing it—
Like to a tenement or pelting farm. 60
England, bound in with the triumphant sea, 61
Whose rocky shore beats back the envious siege
Of wat'ry Neptune, is now bound in with shame, 63
With inky blots and rotten parchment bonds. 64
That England that was wont to conquer others
Hath made a shameful conquest of itself.
Ah, would the scandal vanish with my life,
How happy then were my ensuing death! 68

Enter King [Richard] and Queen, [Aumerle,
Bushy, Green, Bagot, Ross, and Willoughby,] etc.

YORK
The King is come. Deal mildly with his youth,
For young hot colts being reined do rage the more.

QUEEN
How fares our noble uncle Lancaster?

KING RICHARD
What comfort, man? How is't with agèd Gaunt?

GAUNT
Oh, how that name befits my composition! 73
Old Gaunt indeed, and gaunt in being old.
Within me grief hath kept a tedious fast,
And who abstains from meat that is not gaunt? 76
For sleeping England long time have I watched; 77
Watching breeds leanness, leanness is all gaunt.
The pleasure that some fathers feed upon
Is my strict fast—I mean, my children's looks— 80
And, therein fasting, hast thou made me gaunt. 81
Gaunt am I for the grave, gaunt as a grave,
Whose hollow womb inherits naught but bones. 83

possess

84 **nicely** (1) ingeniously (2) triflingly

85 **to mock** of mocking

86–7 **Since . . . thee** Since you seek to destroy my family
name (by banishing my son), I mock my name to
please you and flatter your greatness.

88 **flatter with** try to please

89 **flatter** i.e., are attentive to, offer comfort to

94 **Ill . . . ill** seeing myself to be physically ill, and seeing
the illness in you of abusing your royal authority.

99 **physicians** i.e., the King's favorites

101 **compass** circle, circumference

102 **verge** (1) circle, ring (2) the compass about the King's
court, which extended for twelve miles

103 **waste** (1) waist, circumference (2) that which is destroyed. (With a quibble on the legal meaning of *waste*,
"damage done to property by a tenant.")   **whit** bit,
speck

104 **grandsire** i.e., Edward III

105 **destroy his sons** (1) destroy Edward III's sons,
Richard's uncles (2) destroy Richard's own heritage

106 **From . . . shame** he would have put the matter you
have shamefully handled out of your reach

107 **Deposing** dispossessing.   **possessed** put in possession of the crown

108 **Which . . . thyself** you who are now seized with an
obsessive desire to give away your authority (by leasing
the realm to favorites).

109 **cousin** kinsman, nephew.   **regent** ruler

KING RICHARD

  Can sick men play so nicely with their names?   84

GAUNT

  No, misery makes sport to mock itself.   85
  Since thou dost seek to kill my name in me,   86
  I mock my name, great King, to flatter thee.   87

KING RICHARD

  Should dying men flatter with those that live?   88

GAUNT

  No, no, men living flatter those that die.   89

KING RICHARD

  Thou, now a-dying, sayest thou flatterest me.

GAUNT

  Oh, no, thou diest, though I the sicker be.

KING RICHARD

  I am in health, I breathe, and see thee ill.

GAUNT

  Now He that made me knows I see thee ill;
  Ill in myself to see, and in thee seeing ill.   94
  Thy deathbed is no lesser than thy land,
  Wherein thou liest in reputation sick;
  And thou, too careless patient as thou art,
  Commit'st thy anointed body to the cure
  Of those physicians that first wounded thee.   99
  A thousand flatterers sit within thy crown,
  Whose compass is no bigger than thy head,   101
  And yet, encagèd in so small a verge,   102
  The waste is no whit lesser than thy land.   103
  Oh, had thy grandsire with a prophet's eye   104
  Seen how his son's son should destroy his sons,   105
  From forth thy reach he would have laid thy shame,   106
  Deposing thee before thou wert possessed,   107
  Which art possessed now to depose thyself.   108
  Why, cousin, wert thou regent of the world,   109

111 **But . . . land** i.e., but since you enjoy as your domain
only this land of England (rather than the whole
world)

113 **Landlord** i.e., One who leases out property

114 **Thy . . . to the law** i.e., Your legal status as King is
now subservient to and at the mercy of the law governing contracts, such as blank charters

116 **an ague's privilege** i.e., a sick person's right to be
testy

117 **frozen** (1) chilly (2) caused by a chill

119 **his** its

120 **seat's** throne's

121 **great Edward's son** Edward the Black Prince,
Richard's father

122–3 **runs . . . run** runs on, talks . . . drive, chase

122 **roundly** unceremoniously, bluntly

123 **unreverent** irreverent, disrespectful

125 **For that** simply because

126 **pelican** (The pelican was thought to feed its ungrate-
ful and murderous young with its own blood.)

127 **tapped out** drawn as from a tapped barrel.   **caroused**
gulped, quaffed.

129 **Whom fair befall** to whom may good come

131 **thou respect'st not** you care nothing about

132–4 **Join . . . flower!** May your unnatural behavior act in
concert with my present illness and my advanced years
to cut down my life like a too-long-withered flower!
(*Unkindness* means both cruelty and behavior contrary
to the natural bond that should exist in blood ties.)

135 **die . . . thee** i.e., may your shame live after you.

138 **Love they** Let them desire

139 **sullens** sullenness, melancholy

140 **become** suit

It were a shame to let this land by lease;
But, for thy world enjoying but this land,   111
Is it not more than shame to shame it so?
Landlord of England art thou now, not king.   113
Thy state of law is bondslave to the law,   114
And thou—

KING RICHARD   A lunatic lean-witted fool,
    Presuming on an ague's privilege,   116
    Darest with thy frozen admonition   117
    Make pale our cheek, chasing the royal blood
    With fury from his native residence.   119
    Now, by my seat's right royal majesty,   120
    Wert thou not brother to great Edward's son,   121
    This tongue that runs so roundly in thy head   122
    Should run thy head from thy unreverent shoulders.   123

GAUNT
    Oh, spare me not, my brother Edward's son,
    For that I was his father Edward's son!   125
    That blood already, like the pelican,   126
    Hast thou tapped out and drunkenly caroused.   127
    My brother Gloucester, plain well-meaning soul—
    Whom fair befall in heaven 'mongst happy souls!—   129
    May be a precedent and witness good
    That thou respect'st not spilling Edward's blood.   131
    Join with the present sickness that I have,   132
    And thy unkindness be like crooked age   133
    To crop at once a too-long-withered flower!—   134
    Live in thy shame, but die not shame with thee!   135
    These words hereafter thy tormentors be!—
    Convey me to my bed, then to my grave.
    Love they to live that love and honor have.   138

Exit [borne off by his attendants].

KING RICHARD
    And let them die that age and sullens have,   139
    For both hast thou, and both become the grave.   140

144 **As** i.e., as he would love. (But see the next note.)

145 **Right . . . his** (Richard deliberately takes the opposite of what York had intended to say; Richard gibes that Gaunt is as little fond of the King as is Hereford.)

152 **Though . . . woe** Though death is the privation of life, it does end the misery of human existence which is itself a kind of death in life.

154 **our . . . be** i.e., our journey through life is yet to be completed but will also end.

156–8 **We . . . live** We must expel these shaggy-haired light-armed Irish foot soldiers, who live there like poisonous snakes where no others are allowed to exist. (Richard alludes to the freedom of Ireland from snakes, traditionally ascribed to Saint Patrick.)

159 **for** because.   **ask some charge** require some expenditure

161 **movables** personal property

YORK
I do beseech Your Majesty, impute his words
To wayward sickliness and age in him.
He loves you, on my life, and holds you dear
As Harry Duke of Hereford, were he here.   144

KING RICHARD
Right, you say true. As Hereford's love, so his;   145
As theirs, so mine; and all be as it is.

[*Enter Northumberland.*]

NORTHUMBERLAND
My liege, old Gaunt commends him to Your Majesty.

KING RICHARD
What says he?

NORTHUMBERLAND   Nay, nothing, all is said.
His tongue is now a stringless instrument;
Words, life, and all, old Lancaster hath spent.

YORK
Be York the next that must be bankrupt so!
Though death be poor, it ends a mortal woe.   152

KING RICHARD
The ripest fruit first fails, and so doth he;
His time is spent, our pilgrimage must be.   154
So much for that. Now for our Irish wars:
We must supplant those rough rug-headed kerns,   156
Which live like venom where no venom else   157
But only they have privilege to live.   158
And, for these great affairs do ask some charge,   159
Towards our assistance we do seize to us
The plate, coin, revenues, and movables   161
Whereof our uncle Gaunt did stand possessed.

YORK
How long shall I be patient? Ah, how long
Shall tender duty make me suffer wrong?
Not Gloucester's death, nor Hereford's banishment,

166 **Nor . . . wrongs** nor the rebukes given to Gaunt, nor wrongs inflicted on private English subjects

167–8 **prevention . . . marriage** (Holinshed's *Chronicles* report that Richard had forestalled Bolingbroke's intended marriage with the Duke de Berri's daughter.)

170 **bend . . . on** once frown at the King, or give him reason to frown

173 **was . . . fierce** never was there a lion more fiercely enraged

177 **Accomplished . . . hours** i.e., when he was your age

182 **kindred blood** blood of one's relatives

185 **compare between** draw comparisons.

187 **pleased** satisfied

188 **withal** with that, nonetheless.

190 **royalties** privileges granted through the King and belonging, in this case, to a member of the royal family

195 **Take . . . and take** i.e., If you take . . . you take

196 **His** Time's

197 **ensue** follow

Nor Gaunt's rebukes, nor England's private wrongs,   166
Nor the prevention of poor Bolingbroke   167
About his marriage, nor my own disgrace,   168
Have ever made me sour my patient cheek
Or bend one wrinkle on my sovereign's face.   170
I am the last of noble Edward's sons,
Of whom thy father, Prince of Wales, was first.
In war was never lion raged more fierce,   173
In peace was never gentle lamb more mild,
Than was that young and princely gentleman.
His face thou hast, for even so looked he,
Accomplished with the number of thy hours;   177
But when he frowned, it was against the French
And not against his friends. His noble hand
Did win what he did spend, and spent not that
Which his triumphant father's hand had won.
His hands were guilty of no kindred blood,   182
But bloody with the enemies of his kin.
Oh, Richard! York is too far gone with grief,
Or else he never would compare between.   185

KING RICHARD
Why, uncle, what's the matter?

YORK   O my liege,
Pardon me, if you please; if not, I, pleased   187
Not to be pardoned, am content withal.   188
Seek you to seize and grip into your hands
The royalties and rights of banished Hereford?   190
Is not Gaunt dead? And doth not Hereford live?
Was not Gaunt just? And is not Harry true?
Did not the one deserve to have an heir?
Is not his heir a well-deserving son?
Take Hereford's rights away, and take from Time   195
His charters and his customary rights;   196
Let not tomorrow then ensue today;   197
Be not thyself; for how art thou a king

202–4 Call . . . livery i.e., revoke the royal grant giving him the privilege to sue through his attorneys for possession of his inheritance

204 deny refuse.   **homage** avowal of allegiance (by which ceremony Bolingbroke would be able legally to secure his inheritance)

207 prick i.e., incite

211 by nearby, present

213 by concerning.   **may** it may

214 events outcomes

215 Earl of Wiltshire (The King's Lord Treasurer and one of his notorious favorites.)

216 repair come

217 see see to.   **Tomorrow next** Tomorrow

218 trow believe.

223.2 *Manet* He remains on stage

But by fair sequence and succession?
Now, afore God—God forbid I say true!—
If you do wrongfully seize Hereford's rights,
Call in the letters patents that he hath   202
By his attorneys general to sue   203
His livery, and deny his offered homage,   204
You pluck a thousand dangers on your head,
You lose a thousand well disposèd hearts,
And prick my tender patience to those thoughts   207
Which honor and allegiance cannot think.

KING RICHARD
  Think what you will, we seize into our hands
  His plate, his goods, his money, and his lands.

YORK
  I'll not be by the while. My liege, farewell.   211
  What will ensue hereof there's none can tell;
  But by bad courses may be understood   213
  That their events can never fall out good.   *Exit.*   214

KING RICHARD
  Go, Bushy, to the Earl of Wiltshire straight.   215
  Bid him repair to us to Ely House   216
  To see this business. Tomorrow next   217
  We will for Ireland, and 'tis time, I trow.   218
  And we create, in absence of ourself,
  Our uncle York Lord Governor of England,
  For he is just and always loved us well.—
  Come on, our queen. Tomorrow must we part.
  Be merry, for our time of stay is short.   223
     [*Flourish.*] *Exeunt King and Queen* [*with attendants*].
     Manet Northumberland [*with Willoughby and Ross*].

NORTHUMBERLAND
  Well, lords, the Duke of Lancaster is dead.

ROSS
  And living too, for now his son is duke.

228 **great** i.e., great with sorrow
229 **liberal** unrestrained, freely speaking
230 **ne'er speak more** i.e., die
232 **Tends . . . to** Does what you wish to say concern
237 **gelded** i.e., deprived. (Literally, castrated.)
239 **In him** in his case, or, by him
242 **inform** charge, report as spies
243 **Merely in hate** out of pure hatred
246 **pilled** plundered

WILLOUGHBY

Barely in title, not in revenues.

NORTHUMBERLAND

Richly in both, if justice had her right.

ROSS

My heart is great, but it must break with silence,   228

Ere't be disburdened with a liberal tongue.   229

NORTHUMBERLAND

Nay, speak thy mind; and let him ne'er speak more   230

That speaks thy words again to do thee harm!

WILLOUGHBY

Tends that thou wouldst speak to the Duke of
    Hereford?   232

If it be so, out with it boldly, man.

Quick is mine ear to hear of good towards him.

ROSS

No good at all that I can do for him,

Unless you call it good to pity him,

Bereft and gelded of his patrimony.   237

NORTHUMBERLAND

Now, afore God, 'tis shame such wrongs are borne

In him, a royal prince, and many more   239

Of noble blood in this declining land.

The King is not himself, but basely led

By flatterers; and what they will inform   242

Merely in hate 'gainst any of us all,   243

That will the King severely prosecute

'Gainst us, our lives, our children, and our heirs.

ROSS

The commons hath he pilled with grievous taxes,   246

And quite lost their hearts; the nobles hath he fined

For ancient quarrels, and quite lost their hearts.

250 **blanks** blank charters.   **benevolences** forced loans
to the crown (not actually employed until considerably
later, in 1473).   **wot** know

251 **this** i.e., this unjustly collected revenue.

256 **in farm** on lease.

257 **broken** financially ruined

265 **sore** sorely, grievously

266 **strike** (1) furl the sails (2) strike blows.   **securely**
heedlessly, overconfidently

267 **wrack** ruin

268 **unavoided** unavoidable

269 **suffering** permitting

270 **eyes** eye sockets

WILLOUGHBY

And daily new exactions are devised, *know*

As blanks, benevolences, and I wot not what.   250

But what i' God's name doth become of this?   251

NORTHUMBERLAND

Wars hath not wasted it, for warred he hath not,

But basely yielded upon compromise

That which his noble ancestors achieved with blows.

More hath he spent in peace than they in wars.

ROSS

The Earl of Wiltshire hath the realm in farm.   256

WILLOUGHBY

The King's grown bankrupt, like a broken man.   257

NORTHUMBERLAND

Reproach and dissolution hangeth over him.

ROSS

He hath not money for these Irish wars,

His burdenous taxations notwithstanding,

But by the robbing of the banished Duke.

NORTHUMBERLAND

His noble kinsman. Most degenerate king!

But, lords, we hear this fearful tempest sing,

Yet seek no shelter to avoid the storm;   *grievously*

We see the wind sit sore upon our sails,   265

And yet we strike not, but securely perish.   266

ROSS

We see the very wrack that we must suffer,   267

And unavoided is the danger now   268

For suffering so the causes of our wrack.   269

NORTHUMBERLAND

Not so. Even through the hollow eyes of death   270

I spy life peering; but I dare not say

How near the tidings of our comfort is.

280 . . . (A line is probably missing here, perhaps because of
      censorship. From information contained in Holinshed,
      it may have read something like "Thomas, son and heir
      to the Earl of Arundel" or "The son of Richard, Earl of
      Arundel.")

281 **late broke from** lately escaped from the custody of.
      (Holinshed records that "the Earl of Arundel's son,
      named Thomas, which was kept in the Duke of Exeter's
      house, escaped out of the realm . . . and went to his un-
      cle Thomas Arundel, late Archbishop of Canterbury.")

282 **His** i.e., the Earl of Arundel's.   **late** until recently

286 **tall** stately.   **men of war** troops

287 **expedience** expedition, speed

289–90 **stay . . . King** wait until the King departs

292 **Imp out** piece out. (A term from falconry, meaning to
      attach new feathers to a disabled wing of a bird.)

293 **from broking pawn** from being pledged to pawn-
      brokers

294 **gilt** gold (with pun on *guilt*)

296 **post** haste.   **Ravenspurgh** on the Yorkshire coast,
      at the mouth of the Humber River

297 **faint** are fainthearted

300 **Hold . . . and** If my horse holds out

WILLOUGHBY

Nay, let us share thy thoughts, as thou dost ours.

ROSS

Be confident to speak, Northumberland.
We three are but thyself, and speaking so
Thy words are but as thoughts. Therefore be bold.

NORTHUMBERLAND

Then thus: I have from Port le Blanc,
A bay in Brittany, received intelligence
That Harry Duke of Hereford, Rainold Lord Cobham,
. . . . 280
That late broke from the Duke of Exeter, 281
His brother, Archbishop late of Canterbury, 282
Sir Thomas Erpingham, Sir John Ramston,
Sir John Norbery, Sir Robert Waterton, and Francis
    Coint,
All these well furnished by the Duke of Brittany
With eight tall ships, three thousand men of war, 286
Are making hither with all due expedience 287
And shortly mean to touch our northern shore.
Perhaps they had ere this, but that they stay 289
The first departing of the King for Ireland. 290
If then we shall shake off our slavish yoke,
Imp out our drooping country's broken wing, 292
Redeem from broking pawn the blemished crown, 293
Wipe off the dust that hides our scepter's gilt, 294
And make high majesty look like itself,
Away with me in post to Ravenspurgh; 296
But if you faint, as fearing to do so, 297
Stay and be secret, and myself will go.

ROSS

To horse, to horse! Urge doubts to them that fear.

WILLOUGHBY

Hold out my horse, and I will first be there.   *Exeunt.* 300

2.2 *Location: The court.* (**According to Holinshed, the Queen remained at Windsor Castle when Richard left for Ireland.**)

2 **with** from

3 **heaviness** melancholy

4 **entertain** put on

14 **Each . . . shadows** i.e., For every real grief there exist twenty imagined ones

17 **thing entire to** complete thing into

18 **perspectives** (In lines 16–17, Bushy seems to have in mind a glass with a multifaceted lens, multiplying images of the object being viewed; in lines 18–20, *perspectives* are pictures of figures made to appear distorted or confused, except when viewed obliquely, *eyed awry.*) **rightly** directly, straight

19 **awry** obliquely

20 **Distinguish form** make the form distinct and normal.

21 **awry** i.e., mistakenly, distortedly

22 **himself** i.e., the grief itself.   **wail** bewail

❦ *Enter the Queen, Bushy, [and] Bagot.*

BUSHY

Madam, Your Majesty is too much sad.
You promised, when you parted with the King,   2
To lay aside life-harming heaviness   3
And entertain a cheerful disposition.   4

QUEEN

To please the King I did; to please myself
I cannot do it. Yet I know no cause
Why I should welcome such a guest as grief,
Save bidding farewell to so sweet a guest
As my sweet Richard. Yet again methinks
Some unborn sorrow ripe in Fortune's womb
Is coming towards me, and my inward soul
With nothing trembles. At something it grieves
More than with parting from my lord the King.

BUSHY

Each substance of a grief hath twenty shadows,   14
Which shows like grief itself but is not so;
For sorrow's eyes, glazèd with blinding tears,
Divides one thing entire to many objects,   17
Like perspectives, which rightly gazed upon   18
Show nothing but confusion, eyed awry   19
Distinguish form. So your sweet Majesty,   20
Looking awry upon your lord's departure,   21
Find shapes of grief more than himself to wail,   22
Which, looked on as it is, is naught but shadows
Of what it is not. Then, thrice-gracious Queen,
More than your lord's departure weep not. More is
   not seen,

27 **for** in place of.   **weeps** weeps for

31–2 **As . . . shrink** that, though I seem to be thinking of nothing, my "nothing" is so *heavy* or saddening that I faint and fall back under the weight.

33 **conceit** fancy

34 **'Tis nothing less** i.e., It is anything but that.   **still** always

36 **something** i.e., substantial

37 **something . . . grieve** the unsubstantial grief, the nothing, that I grieve about has something to it, some substance.

38–40 **'Tis . . . name** i.e., My grief is like a legacy that will come to me at some future time, but I cannot tell its nature yet.

40 **wot** know, assume.

44 **For . . . hope** for his plans require that he proceed expeditiously to Ireland, and that his haste will bring hope of good success.

46 **retired his power** held back his army (in order to be able to repulse Bolingbroke's landing)

49 **repeals** recalls (from exile)

50 **uplifted arms** weapons raised in rebellion

Or if it be, 'tis with false sorrow's eye,
Which for things true weeps things imaginary. 27

QUEEN
It may be so, but yet my inward soul
Persuades me it is otherwise. Howe'er it be,
I cannot but be sad—so heavy sad
As, though on thinking on no thought I think, 31
Makes me with heavy nothing faint and shrink. 32

BUSHY
'Tis nothing but conceit, my gracious lady. 33

QUEEN
'Tis nothing less. Conceit is still derived 34
From some forefather grief. Mine is not so,
For nothing hath begot my something grief, 36
Or something hath the nothing that I grieve. 37
'Tis in reversion that I do possess; 38
But what it is, that is not yet known what, 39
I cannot name. 'Tis nameless woe, I wot. 40

[Enter Green.]

GREEN
God save Your Majesty! And well met, gentlemen.
I hope the King is not yet shipped for Ireland.

QUEEN
Why hopest thou so? 'Tis better hope he is,
For his designs crave haste, his haste good hope. 44
Then wherefore dost thou hope he is not shipped?

GREEN
That he, our hope, might have retired his power, 46
And driven into despair an enemy's hope,
Who strongly hath set footing in this land.
The banished Bolingbroke repeals himself 49
And with uplifted arms is safe arrived 50
At Ravenspurgh.

52 **that** what

57 **rest** rest of the

59 **broken his staff** broken his badge of office (in token of
resignation as Lord High Steward. Worcester is brother
of the Earl of Northumberland.)

63 **dismal heir** ill-omened offspring.

64 **prodigy** monstrous birth

69 **cozening** cheating.   **He** i.e., False hope

71 **Who** i.e., death

72 **lingers** causes to linger

74 **signs of war** i.e., a piece of armor called the gorget, an
iron collar that could be worn with ordinary clothes

QUEEN   Now God in heaven forbid!

GREEN
  Ah, madam, 'tis too true; and that is worse,   52
  The lord Northumberland, his son young Harry
     Percy,
  The lords of Ross, Beaumont, and Willoughby,
  With all their powerful friends, are fled to him.

BUSHY
  Why have you not proclaimed Northumberland
  And all the rest revolted faction traitors?   57

GREEN
  We have, whereupon the Earl of Worcester
  Hath broken his staff, resigned his stewardship,   59
  And all the household servants fled with him
  To Bolingbroke.

QUEEN
  So, Green, thou art the midwife to my woe,
  And Bolingbroke my sorrow's dismal heir.   63
  Now hath my soul brought forth her prodigy,   64
  And I, a gasping new-delivered mother,
  Have woe to woe, sorrow to sorrow joined.

BUSHY
  Despair not, madam.

QUEEN   Who shall hinder me?
  I will despair, and be at enmity
  With cozening hope. He is a flatterer,   69
  A parasite, a keeper-back of death
  Who gently would dissolve the bonds of life   71
  Which false hope lingers in extremity.   72

    [Enter York.]

GREEN   Here comes the Duke of York.

QUEEN
  With signs of war about his agèd neck.   74

75 **careful business** worried preoccupation

76 **comfortable** affording comfort

79 **crosses** obstacles, obstructions

80 **save far off** i.e., defend his rule in Ireland

82 **underprop** prop up, support

85 **try** test

86 **your son** i.e., the Duke of Aumerle

90 **Sirrah** (Said to inferiors.) **sister** sister-in-law

91 **presently** immediately

92 **ring** (By which the Duchess will know that the request is sent by York himself.)

96 **knave** i.e., fellow.

Oh, full of careful business are his looks!   75
Uncle, for God's sake, speak comfortable words.   76

YORK

Should I do so, I should belie my thoughts.
Comfort's in heaven, and we are on the earth,
Where nothing lives but crosses, cares, and grief.   79
Your husband, he is gone to save far off,   80
Whilst others come to make him lose at home.
Here am I left to underprop his land,   82
Who, weak with age, cannot support myself.
Now comes the sick hour that his surfeit made;
Now shall he try his friends that flattered him.   85

[Enter a Servingman.]

SERVINGMAN

My lord, your son was gone before I came.   86

YORK

He was? Why, so. Go all which way it will!
The nobles they are fled, the commons they are cold,
And will, I fear, revolt on Hereford's side.
Sirrah, get thee to Pleshey, to my sister Gloucester;   90
Bid her send me presently a thousand pound.   91
Hold, take my ring.   92

SERVINGMAN

My lord, I had forgot to tell Your Lordship:
Today, as I came by, I callèd there—
But I shall grieve you to report the rest.

YORK   What is't, knave?   96

SERVINGMAN

An hour before I came, the Duchess died.

YORK

God for his mercy, what a tide of woes
Comes rushing on this woeful land at once!
I know not what to do. I would to God,

101 **So my untruth** provided that some disloyalty on my part

102 **brother's** i.e., the Duke of Gloucester's.

115 **my . . . right** my kinship to him bids that I right his wrong.

116 **somewhat** something.   **cousin** i.e., the Queen

117 **dispose of** make arrangements for

119 **Berkeley** a castle near Bristol.

121 **at six and seven** i.e., in confusion.

121.2 *Manent* They remain on stage

127 **Is . . . King** makes us enemies of those who oppose the King.

So my untruth had not provoked him to it,   101
The King had cut off my head with my brother's.   102
What, are there no posts dispatched for Ireland?
How shall we do for money for these wars?
Come, sister—cousin, I would say—pray pardon
    me.—
Go, fellow, get thee home. Provide some carts
And bring away the armor that is there.

                              [*Exit Servingman.*]

Gentlemen, will you go muster men?
If I know how or which way to order these affairs
Thus disorderly thrust into my hands,
Never believe me. Both are my kinsmen:
Th'one is my sovereign, whom both my oath
And duty bids defend; t'other again
Is my kinsman, whom the King hath wronged,
Whom conscience and my kindred bids to right.   115
Well, somewhat we must do.—Come, cousin,   116
I'll dispose of you.—Gentlemen,   117
Go, muster up your men, and meet me presently
At Berkeley. I should to Pleshey too,   119
But time will not permit. All is uneven,
And everything is left at six and seven.   121

                    Exeunt Duke [*of York*], *Queen.*
                    Manent Bushy, [*Bagot,*] *Green.*

BUSHY
    The wind sits fair for news to go to Ireland,
    But none returns. For us to levy power
    Proportionable to the enemy
    Is all unpossible.

GREEN
    Besides, our nearness to the King in love
    Is near the hate of those love not the King.   127

BAGOT
    And that is the wavering commons, for their love

132 **If . . . we** i.e., If the power to pass judgment is given
to the wavering commons, then we, too, stand condemned

133 **ever** always

136 **office** service

137 **hateful** full of hate, angry

141 **vain** in vain

143 **That's . . . thrives** i.e., That depends upon York's efforts and success

Lies in their purses, and whoso empties them
By so much fills their hearts with deadly hate.

BUSHY

Wherein the King stands generally condemned.

BAGOT

If judgment lie in them, then so do we,   132
Because we ever have been near the King.   133

GREEN

Well, I will for refuge straight to Bristol Castle.
The Earl of Wiltshire is already there.

BUSHY

Thither will I with you, for little office   136
Will the hateful commons perform for us,   137
Except like curs to tear us all to pieces.
[*To Bagot*] Will you go along with us?

BAGOT

No, I will to Ireland to His Majesty.
Farewell. If heart's presages be not vain,   141
We three here part that ne'er shall meet again.

BUSHY

That's as York thrives to beat back Bolingbroke.   143

GREEN

Alas, poor duke! The task he undertakes
Is numbering sands and drinking oceans dry.
Where one on his side fights, thousands will fly.
Farewell at once, for once, for all, and ever.

BUSHY

Well, we may meet again.

BAGOT   I fear me, never.

                                          [*Exeunt.*]

2.3 *Location: In Gloucestershire, near Berkeley Castle.*

9 **Cotswold** hilly district in Gloucestershire

10 **In** by.   **wanting** lacking

11 **protest** declare

12 **tediousness and process** tedious process

15–16 **And hope . . . enjoyed** and the hope of future happiness is only slightly less joyous than happiness already
enjoyed.

16 **this** this expectation

22 **whencesoever** from wherever he is.

23 **your uncle** i.e., the Earl of Worcester.

[2.3] ⍞ *Enter [Bolingbroke, Duke of] Hereford, [and] Northumberland [with forces].*

BOLINGBROKE
    How far is it, my lord, to Berkeley now?

NORTHUMBERLAND   Believe me, noble lord,
    I am a stranger here in Gloucestershire.
    These high wild hills and rough uneven ways
    Draws out our miles and makes them wearisome,
    And yet your fair discourse hath been as sugar,
    Making the hard way sweet and delectable.
    But I bethink me what a weary way
    From Ravenspurgh to Cotswold will be found   9
    In Ross and Willoughby, wanting your company,   10
    Which, I protest, hath very much beguiled   11
    The tediousness and process of my travel.   12
    But theirs is sweetened with the hope to have
    The present benefit which I possess;
    And hope to joy is little less in joy   15
    Than hope enjoyed. By this the weary lords   16
    Shall make their way seem short, as mine hath done
    By sight of what I have: your noble company.

BOLINGBROKE
    Of much less value is my company
    Than your good words. But who comes here?

        Enter Harry Percy.

NORTHUMBERLAND
    It is my son, young Harry Percy,
    Sent from my brother Worcester whencesoever.—   22
    Harry, how fares your uncle?   23

34 **power** troops

35 **directions** instructions.   **repair** go

36 **boy** (A rebuke for not respectfully greeting Bolingbroke, though historically Percy was two years Bolingbroke's senior.)

41 **tender** offer. (With a pun in the next line on the meaning "inexperienced.")   **my service** (Presumably Percy kneels to Bolingbroke, and so do Ross and Willoughby when they enter.)

44 **approvèd** proven, demonstrated

47 **in a** in my

PERCY

    I had thought, my lord, to have learned his health of
        you.

NORTHUMBERLAND   Why, is he not with the Queen?

PERCY

    No, my good lord. He hath forsook the court,
    Broken his staff of office, and dispersed
    The household of the King.

NORTHUMBERLAND   What was his reason?

    He was not so resolved when last we spake together.

PERCY

    Because Your Lordship was proclaimèd traitor.
    But he, my lord, is gone to Ravenspurgh
    To offer service to the Duke of Hereford,
    And sent me over by Berkeley to discover
    What power the Duke of York had levied there,   34
    Then with directions to repair to Ravenspurgh.   35

NORTHUMBERLAND

    Have you forgot the Duke of Hereford, boy?   36

PERCY

    No, my good lord, for that is not forgot
    Which ne'er I did remember. To my knowledge
    I never in my life did look on him.

NORTHUMBERLAND

    Then learn to know him now. This is the Duke.

PERCY

    My gracious lord, I tender you my service,   41
    Such as it is, being tender, raw, and young,
    Which elder days shall ripen and confirm
    To more approvèd service and desert.   44

BOLINGBROKE

    I thank thee, gentle Percy, and be sure
    I count myself in nothing else so happy
    As in a soul rememb'ring my good friends;   47

48–9 **And . . . recompense** and as my fortunes improve, assisted by your loyalty to me, I will be increasingly enabled to reward you for that loyalty.

51 **stir** action

56 **estimate** rank.

58 **spurring** i.e., hard riding

59 **wot** am aware that. (Bolingbroke graciously indicates his awareness of the risk they are taking in supporting him.)

61 **unfelt** impalpable, expressed in words, not gifts.   **which** i.e., which treasury.   **more enriched** i.e., with still more thanks added, or, with substantial gifts at a later date

65 **Evermore . . . poor** "Thank you" is always the exchequer of the poor, i.e., the only means they have to repay favors

66 **comes to years** reaches maturity

67 **Stands for** serves in place of

And as my fortune ripens with thy love,   48
It shall be still thy true love's recompense.   49
My heart this covenant makes, my hand thus seals it.

               [He offers Percy his hand.]

NORTHUMBERLAND
How far is it to Berkeley? And what stir   51
Keeps good old York there with his men of war?

PERCY
There stands the castle by yon tuft of trees,
Manned with three hundred men, as I have heard,
And in it are the lords of York, Berkeley, and Seymour,
None else of name and noble estimate.   56

    [Enter Ross and Willoughby.]

NORTHUMBERLAND
Here come the lords of Ross and Willoughby,
Bloody with spurring, fiery red with haste.   58

BOLINGBROKE
Welcome, my lords. I wot your love pursues   59
A banished traitor. All my treasury
Is yet but unfelt thanks, which, more enriched,   61
Shall be your love and labor's recompense.

ROSS
Your presence makes us rich, most noble lord.

WILLOUGHBY
And far surmounts our labor to attain it.

BOLINGBROKE
Evermore thank's the exchequer of the poor,   65
Which, till my infant fortune comes to years,   66
Stands for my bounty. But who comes here?   67

    [Enter Berkeley.]

NORTHUMBERLAND
It is my lord of Berkeley, as I guess.

70 **"Lancaster"** (Bolingbroke will enter into no negotiations unless his proper title, taken away by Richard, is
given him.)

75 **raze** scrape (or perhaps *rase*, "erase")

76 **what . . . will** whatever title you prefer to be addressed
by. (Said sardonically.)

78 **pricks** spurs

79 **the absent time** i.e., the time of the King's absence

80 **self-borne** borne in your own private cause, not the
country's welfare. (Also suggesting *self-born*, "originat-
ing in the self.")

84 **duty** gesture of obeisance.   **deceivable** deceitful, de-
ceptive

91 **dust** particle of dust

95 **ostentation** display.   **despisèd** despicable

BERKELEY
My lord of Hereford, my message is to you.

BOLINGBROKE
My lord, my answer is—to "Lancaster";   70
And I am come to seek that name in England,
And I must find that title in your tongue
Before I make reply to aught you say.

BERKELEY
Mistake me not, my lord, 'tis not my meaning
To raze one title of your honor out.   75
To you, my lord, I come, what lord you will,   76
From the most gracious regent of this land,
The Duke of York, to know what pricks you on   78
To take advantage of the absent time   79
And fright our native peace with self-borne arms.   80

[*Enter York.*]

BOLINGBROKE
I shall not need transport my words by you;
Here comes His Grace in person.—My noble uncle!
[*He kneels.*]

YORK
Show me thy humble heart, and not thy knee,
Whose duty is deceivable and false.   84

BOLINGBROKE   My gracious uncle—

YORK   Tut, tut!
Grace me no grace, nor uncle me no uncle.
I am no traitor's uncle; and that word "grace"
In an ungracious mouth is but profane.
Why have those banished and forbidden legs
Dared once to touch a dust of England's ground?   91
But then more "why?" Why have they dared to march
So many miles upon her peaceful bosom,
Frighting her pale-faced villages with war
And ostentation of despisèd arms?   95

101 **the Black Prince** i.e., Edward, the eldest son of Edward III and King Richard's father

105 **minister** administer

107 **condition** defect in me, or provision of the law. **wherein** in what does it consist.

112 **braving** (1) defiant (2) defiantly brandishing. (Also at line 143.)

114 **for Lancaster** i.e., under the title of Lancaster and in order to claim it.

116 **indifferent** impartial

119 **condemned** condemned as

120 **royalties** privileges granted by the King

122 **unthrifts** spendthrifts.

126 **first** i.e., before Gaunt

Com'st thou because the anointed King is hence?
Why, foolish boy, the King is left behind,
And in my loyal bosom lies his power.
Were I but now the lord of such hot youth
As when brave Gaunt, thy father, and myself
Rescued the Black Prince, that young Mars of men,   101
From forth the ranks of many thousand French,
Oh, then how quickly should this arm of mine,
Now prisoner to the palsy, chastise thee
And minister correction to thy fault!   105

BOLINGBROKE

My gracious uncle, let me know my fault.
On what condition stands it and wherein?   107

YORK

Even in condition of the worst degree:
In gross rebellion and detested treason.
Thou art a banished man, and here art come
Before the expiration of thy time
In braving arms against thy sovereign.   112

BOLINGBROKE [*standing*]

As I was banished, I was banished Hereford;
But as I come, I come for Lancaster.   114
And, noble uncle, I beseech Your Grace
Look on my wrongs with an indifferent eye.   116
You are my father, for methinks in you
I see old Gaunt alive. Oh, then, my father,
Will you permit that I shall stand condemned   119
A wandering vagabond, my rights and royalties   120
Plucked from my arms perforce and given away
To upstart unthrifts? Wherefore was I born?   122
If that my cousin king be King in England,
It must be granted I am Duke of Lancaster.
You have a son, Aumerle, my noble cousin;
Had you first died, and he been thus trod down,   126

128 **rouse** chase from cover, expose. **the bay** the extremity where the hunted animal turns on its pursuers.

129 **I am . . . here** I am denied the right to sue for possession of hereditary rights in England. (See 2.1.202–4 and
note.)

130 **letters patents** i.e., letters from the King indicating a
subject's legal rights

131 **distrained** seized officially

134 **challenge law** claim my legal rights.

136 **of free descent** by legal succession.

138 **stands . . . upon** is incumbent upon Your Grace

139 **his endowments** i.e., the properties that rightly
belong to Bolingbroke

141 **cousin's** nephew's

143 **kind** fashion

144 **Be . . . carver** i.e., act on his own authority, help himself

151 **joy** i.e., the joy of heaven

152 **issue** outcome

154 **power** army.   **ill-left** left in dismay and with inade-
quate means

He should have found his uncle Gaunt a father
To rouse his wrongs and chase them to the bay.   128
I am denied to sue my livery here,   129
And yet my letters patents give me leave.   130
My father's goods are all distrained and sold,   131
And these, and all, are all amiss employed.
What would you have me do? I am a subject,
And I challenge law. Attorneys are denied me,   134
And therefore personally I lay my claim
To my inheritance of free descent.   136

NORTHUMBERLAND
The noble Duke hath been too much abused.

ROSS
It stands Your Grace upon to do him right.   138

WILLOUGHBY
Base men by his endowments are made great.   139

YORK
My lords of England, let me tell you this:
I have had feeling of my cousin's wrongs   141
And labored all I could to do him right;
But in this kind to come, in braving arms,   143
Be his own carver, and cut out his way   144
To find out right with wrong—it may not be;
And you that do abet him in this kind
Cherish rebellion and are rebels all.

NORTHUMBERLAND
The noble Duke hath sworn his coming is
But for his own, and for the right of that
We all have strongly sworn to give him aid;
And let him never see joy that breaks that oath!   151

YORK
Well, well, I see the issue of these arms.   152
I cannot mend it, I must needs confess,
Because my power is weak and all ill-left;   154

156 **attach** arrest
159 **as neuter** neutral.
163 **win** persuade
165 **Bagot** (According to 2.2.140, Bagot had gone to Ireland.)
170 **Nor** Neither as

2.4 *Location: A camp in Wales.*
1 **stayed** waited
2 **hardly** with difficulty
3 **yet** still

But if I could, by Him that gave me life,
I would attach you all and make you stoop   156
Unto the sovereign mercy of the King.
But since I cannot, be it known unto you
I do remain as neuter. So fare you well—   159
Unless you please to enter in the castle
And there repose you for this night.

BOLINGBROKE
An offer, uncle, that we will accept.
But we must win Your Grace to go with us   163
To Bristol Castle, which they say is held
By Bushy, Bagot, and their complices,   165
The caterpillars of the commonwealth,
Which I have sworn to weed and pluck away.

YORK
It may be I will go with you; but yet I'll pause,
For I am loath to break our country's laws.
Nor friends nor foes, to me welcome you are.   170
Things past redress are now with me past care.

                                   Exeunt.

[2.4] ❧ *Enter Earl of Salisbury and a Welsh Captain.*

WELSH CAPTAIN
My lord of Salisbury, we have stayed ten days   1
And hardly kept our countrymen together,   2
And yet we hear no tidings from the King.   3
Therefore we will disperse ourselves. Farewell.

SALISBURY
Stay yet another day, thou trusty Welshman.
The King reposeth all his confidence in thee.

WELSH CAPTAIN
'Tis thought the King is dead. We will not stay.
The bay trees in our country are all withered,

11 **lean-looked** lean-looking
14 **to . . . rage** in hopes of possessing by violence
15 **forerun** anticipate
17 **As** as being
22 **Witnessing** betokening
23 **wait upon** attend, offer allegiance to
24 **crossly** adversely

3.1 *Location: Bristol. The castle.*
 3 **presently** immediately
 4 **urging** emphasizing as reasons (for your executions)
 7 **unfold** reveal
 9 **happy** fortunate.   **blood and lineaments** birth and natural characteristics
10 **By . . . clean** by you made wretched and wholly marred in reputation.
11 **in manner** as it were

And meteors fright the fixèd stars of heaven;
The pale-faced moon looks bloody on the earth,
And lean-looked prophets whisper fearful change;   11
Rich men look sad, and ruffians dance and leap,
The one in fear to lose what they enjoy,
The other to enjoy by rage and war.   14
These signs forerun the death or fall of kings.   15
Farewell. Our countrymen are gone and fled,
As well assured Richard their king is dead.   [*Exit.*]   17

SALISBURY
Ah, Richard! With the eyes of heavy mind
I see thy glory like a shooting star
Fall to the base earth from the firmament.
Thy sun sets weeping in the lowly west,
Witnessing storms to come, woe, and unrest.   22
Thy friends are fled to wait upon thy foes,   23
And crossly to thy good all fortune goes.   [*Exit.*]   24

[3.1] ◦ɕ~ *Enter [Bolingbroke,] Duke of Hereford, York,*
          Northumberland, [with] Bushy and Green,
          prisoners.

BOLINGBROKE   Bring forth these men.
Bushy and Green, I will not vex your souls—
Since presently your souls must part your bodies—   3
With too much urging your pernicious lives,   4
For 'twere no charity; yet, to wash your blood
From off my hands, here in the view of men
I will unfold some causes of your deaths.   7
You have misled a prince, a royal king,
A happy gentleman in blood and lineaments,   9
By you unhappied and disfigured clean.   10
You have in manner with your sinful hours   11
Made a divorce betwixt his queen and him,
Broke the possession of a royal bed,

20 **foreign clouds** i.e., the air of foreign lands (and adding to the clouds with sighs)

22 **seigniories** estates

23 **Disparked** thrown open to uses other than hunting and forestry

24 **household coat** coat of arms (frequently emblazoned on stained or painted windows)

25 **Razed** scraped (or perhaps *rased*, "erased"). **imprese** heraldic device, emblematic design

37 **entreated** treated.

38 **commends** regards, compliments.

41 **at large** conveyed in full.

And stained the beauty of a fair queen's cheeks
With tears drawn from her eyes by your foul wrongs.
Myself—a prince by fortune of my birth,
Near to the King in blood, and near in love
Till you did make him misinterpret me—
Have stooped my neck under your injuries
And sighed my English breath in foreign clouds,   20
Eating the bitter bread of banishment,
Whilst you have fed upon my seigniories,   22
Disparked my parks and felled my forest woods,   23
From my own windows torn my household coat,   24
Razed out my imprese, leaving me no sign,   25
Save men's opinions and my living blood,
To show the world I am a gentleman.
This and much more, much more than twice all this,
Condemns you to the death.—See them delivered
     over
To execution and the hand of death.

BUSHY

More welcome is the stroke of death to me
Than Bolingbroke to England. Lords, farewell.

GREEN

My comfort is that heaven will take our souls
And plague injustice with the pains of hell.

BOLINGBROKE

My lord Northumberland, see them dispatched.
     [*Exeunt Northumberland with the prisoners, guarded.*]
Uncle, you say the Queen is at your house.
For God's sake, fairly let her be entreated.   37
Tell her I send to her my kind commends.   38
Take special care my greetings be delivered.

YORK

A gentleman of mine I have dispatched
With letters of your love to her at large.   41

43 **Glendower** (Owen Glendower was not, according to Holinshed's *Chronicles,* at this time in arms against Bolingbroke. Possibly he is to be identified here with the Welsh captain of the preceding scene.)

44 **after** afterwards

3.2 *Location: The coast of Wales, near Harlech Castle.*

1 **Barkloughly** i.e., Harlech

2 **brooks** enjoys

3 **late** recent

4 **Needs must** Necessarily

8 **a long-parted mother with** mother long parted from

13 **sweets** i.e., bounty.   **sense** appetite

14 **suck . . . venom** (Alludes to the belief that spiders drew their poison from the earth.)

15 **heavy-gaited** lumbering, clumsy

21 **double** forked.   **mortal** deadly

BOLINGBROKE

> Thanks, gentle uncle. Come, lords, away,
> To fight with Glendower and his complices.   43
> Awhile to work, and after holiday.   *Exeunt.*   44

[3.2] ❧ *[Drums. Flourish and colors.] Enter the King,*
         Aumerle, [the Bishop of] Carlisle, etc. [with
         soldiers].

KING RICHARD

> Barkloughly Castle call they this at hand?   1

AUMERLE

> Yea, my lord. How brooks Your Grace the air   2
> After your late tossing on the breaking seas?   3

KING RICHARD

> Needs must I like it well. I weep for joy   4
> To stand upon my kingdom once again.
> Dear earth, I do salute thee with my hand,
>
>   *[He bends and touches the ground.]*
>
> Though rebels wound thee with their horses' hoofs.
> As a long-parted mother with her child   8
> Plays fondly with her tears and smiles in meeting,
> So, weeping, smiling, greet I thee, my earth,
> And do thee favors with my royal hands.
> Feed not thy sovereign's foe, my gentle earth,
> Nor with thy sweets comfort his ravenous sense,   13
> But let thy spiders, that suck up thy venom,   14
> And heavy-gaited toads lie in their way,   15
> Doing annoyance to the treacherous feet
> Which with usurping steps do trample thee.
> Yield stinging nettles to mine enemies;
> And when they from thy bosom pluck a flower,
> Guard it, I pray thee, with a lurking adder,
> Whose double tongue may with a mortal touch   21

23 **senseless conjuration** solemn entreaty of senseless
  things; or, one that makes no sense to you, being so fan-
  ciful

25 **native** entitled (to the crown) by birth, rightful. (Richard
  was born at Bordeaux.)

30–1 **else . . . not** i.e., otherwise, we spurn heaven's will.

32 **succor and redress** help and remedy.

34 **security** overconfidence

36 **Discomfortable** Disheartening, discouraging

37–8 **when . . . world** i.e., when the sun is hid behind the
  earth, lighting its lower side

41 **this terrestrial ball** the earth

42 **He fires** the sun lights up. (Literally, "sets on fire.")

46 **at themselves** i.e., at being caught in their crimes.

49 **Antipodes** people on the other side of the world; here,
  the Irish. (A geographical hyperbole.)

Throw death upon thy sovereign's enemies.—
Mock not my senseless conjuration, lords.   23
This earth shall have a feeling, and these stones
Prove armèd soldiers, ere her native king   25
Shall falter under foul rebellion's arms.

CARLISLE
Fear not, my lord. That Power that made you king
Hath power to keep you king in spite of all.
The means that heavens yield must be embraced
And not neglected; else heaven would,   30
And we will not. Heaven's offer we refuse,   31
The proffered means of <u>succor and redress</u>.   32

help and remedy

AUMERLE
He means, my lord, that we are too remiss,
Whilst Bolingbroke through our security   34
Grows strong and great in substance and in power.

KING RICHARD
Discomfortable cousin, know'st thou not   36
That when the searching eye of heaven is hid   37
Behind the globe that lights the lower world,   38
Then thieves and robbers range abroad unseen
In murders and in outrage boldly here;
But when from under this terrestrial ball   41
He fires the proud tops of the eastern pines   42
And darts his light through every guilty hole,
Then murders, treasons, and detested sins,
The cloak of night being plucked from off their backs,
Stand bare and naked, trembling at themselves?   46
So when this thief, this traitor, Bolingbroke,
Who all this while hath reveled in the night
Whilst we were wand'ring with the Antipodes,   49
Shall see us rising in our throne, the east,
His treasons will sit blushing in his face,
Not able to endure the sight of day,
But, self-affrighted, tremble at his sin.

55 **balm** consecrated oil used in anointing a king

56 **worldly** earthly

57 **elected** chosen

58 **pressed** impressed, forced into the ranks

59 **shrewd** keen, biting

62 **still** always

64 **Nor near** Neither nearer

65 **Discomfort** Discouragement

72 **state** royal power

76 **But now** Even now.   **twenty** (A seeming discrepancy with *twelve* in line 70; perhaps the result of Richard's hyperbole.)

77 **triumph** i.e., shine forth

79 **pale and dead** deathly pale.

Not all the water in the rough rude sea
Can wash the balm off from an anointed king;   55
The breath of worldly men cannot depose   56
The deputy elected by the Lord.   57
For every man that Bolingbroke hath pressed   58
To lift shrewd steel against our golden crown,   59
God for his Richard hath in heavenly pay
A glorious angel. Then, if angels fight,
Weak men must fall, for heaven still guards the right.   62

    Enter Salisbury.

Welcome, my lord. How far off lies your power?

SALISBURY
Nor near nor farther off, my gracious lord,   64
Than this weak arm. Discomfort guides my tongue   65
And bids me speak of nothing but despair.
One day too late, I fear me, noble lord,
Hath clouded all thy happy days on earth.
Oh, call back yesterday, bid time return,
And thou shalt have twelve thousand fighting men!
Today, today, unhappy day too late,
O'erthrows thy joys, friends, fortune, and thy state;   72
For all the Welshmen, hearing thou wert dead,
Are gone to Bolingbroke, dispersed, and fled.

AUMERLE
Comfort, my liege. Why looks Your Grace so pale?

KING RICHARD
But now the blood of twenty thousand men   76
    Did triumph in my face, and they are fled;   77
And till so much blood thither come again,
    Have I not reason to look pale and dead?   79

81 **blot** stain

91 **More . . . betide** May more health and happiness befall

92 **care-tuned** i.e., tuned by sorrow and to the key of sorrow.   **deliver** deliver to

94 **unfold** reveal.

95 **care** trouble

99 **his fellow** his (Bolingbroke's) equal

104 **armed** prepared

All souls that will be safe, fly from my side,
For time hath set a blot upon my pride.   81

AUMERLE
Comfort, my liege. Remember who you are.

KING RICHARD
I had forgot myself. Am I not king?
Awake, thou coward majesty, thou sleepest!
Is not the king's name twenty thousand names?
Arm, arm, my name! A puny subject strikes
At thy great glory. Look not to the ground,
Ye favorites of a king. Are we not high?
High be our thoughts. I know my uncle York
Hath power enough to serve our turn. But who comes
    here?

        Enter Scroop.

SCROOP
More health and happiness betide my liege   91
Than can my care-tuned tongue deliver him!   92

KING RICHARD
Mine ear is open and my heart prepared.
The worst is worldly loss thou canst unfold.   94
Say, is my kingdom lost? Why, 'twas my care,   95
And what loss is it to be rid of care?
Strives Bolingbroke to be as great as we?
Greater he shall not be; if he serve God,
We'll serve Him too, and be his fellow so.   99
Revolt our subjects? That we cannot mend;
They break their faith to God as well as us.
Cry woe, destruction, ruin, and decay;
The worst is death, and death will have his day.

SCROOP
Glad am I that Your Highness is so armed   104
To bear the tidings of calamity.
Like an unseasonable stormy day,

109 **his limits** (1) its banks (2) the limits properly allowed
to Bolingbroke's rage

110 **fearful** full of fears

112 **Whitebeards** Old men.   **thin** sparsely haired

114 **Strive . . . joints** strive to speak with deep manlike
voices, and thrust their adolescent limbs

115 **arms** armor

116 **beadsmen** old almsmen or pensioners whose duty it
was to pray for a benefactor; here, for the King

117 **double-fatal** doubly fatal (since the wood of the yew
was used for bows and since its foliage and berries are
poisonous; yews were also commonly planted in grave-
yards)

118–19 **distaff-women . . . seat** spinning women wield
unused and hence rusty pikes (long-handled ax-like
weapons) against your throne.

122 **Bagot** (Although the King names Bagot here, he mentions only *three* Judases in line 132 and Aumerle does
not ask about Bagot in line 141; in 3.4 we learn that
Bagot is not executed along with the other three but
reappears instead in 4.1.)

125 **Measure our confines** travel over my kingdom.
peaceful unopposed

134 **spotted** stained with treason

135 **his property** its distinctive quality

Which makes the silver rivers drown their shores
As if the world were all dissolved to tears,
So high above his limits swells the rage   109
Of Bolingbroke, covering your fearful land   110
With hard bright steel and hearts harder than steel.
Whitebeards have armed their thin and hairless scalps   112
Against Thy Majesty; boys with women's voices
Strive to speak big, and clap their female joints   114
In stiff unwieldy arms against thy crown.   115
Thy very beadsmen learn to bend their bows   116
Of double-fatal yew against thy state;   117
Yea, distaff-women manage rusty bills   118
Against thy seat. Both young and old rebel,   119
And all goes worse than I have power to tell.

KING RICHARD
Too well, too well thou tell'st a tale so ill.
Where is the Earl of Wiltshire? Where is Bagot?   122
What is become of Bushy? Where is Green,
That they have let the dangerous enemy
Measure our confines with such peaceful steps?   125
If we prevail, their heads shall pay for it.
I warrant they have made peace with Bolingbroke.

SCROOP
Peace have they made with him indeed, my lord.

KING RICHARD
Oh, villains, vipers, damned without redemption!
Dogs easily won to fawn on any man!
Snakes in my heart-blood warmed, that sting my
    heart!
Three Judases, each one thrice worse than Judas!
Would they make peace? Terrible hell
Make war upon their spotted souls for this!   134

SCROOP
Sweet love, I see, changing his property,   135
Turns to the sourest and most deadly hate.

138 **hands** (Used in swearing oaths, surrendering, etc.)

140 **graved** buried

150 **deposèd** (1) dethroned, as in 4.1 (2) deprived of those
functions carried out by the body in this transitory life
(3) deposited

153 **model** microcosm or mold, i.e., the body

154 **paste** pastry, pie crust

158 **deposed** deprived of life

161 **rounds** encircles

162 **antic** grotesque figure, jester

163 **Scoffing his state** scoffing at the King's regality

164 **breath** breathing space, moment

165 **monarchize** play the monarch.   **kill with looks** i.e.,
order someone's death with a mere glance

166 **self and vain conceit** vain conceit of himself

Again uncurse their souls. Their peace is made
With heads and not with hands. Those whom you
    curse   138
Have felt the worst of death's destroying wound
And lie full low, graved in the hollow ground.   140

AUMERLE
Is Bushy, Green, and the Earl of Wiltshire dead?

SCROOP
Ay, all of them at Bristol lost their heads.

AUMERLE
Where is the Duke my father with his power?

KING RICHARD
No matter where. Of comfort no man speak!
Let's talk of graves, of worms, and epitaphs,
Make dust our paper, and with rainy eyes
Write sorrow on the bosom of the earth.
Let's choose executors and talk of wills.
And yet not so, for what can we bequeath
Save our deposèd bodies to the ground?   150
Our lands, our lives, and all are Bolingbroke's,
And nothing can we call our own but death
And that small model of the barren earth   153
Which serves as paste and cover to our bones.   154
For God's sake, let us sit upon the ground
And tell sad stories of the death of kings—
How some have been deposed, some slain in war,
Some haunted by the ghosts they have deposed,   158
Some poisoned by their wives, some sleeping killed,
All murdered. For within the hollow crown
That rounds the mortal temples of a king   161
Keeps Death his court, and there the antic sits,   162
Scoffing his state and grinning at his pomp,   163
Allowing him a breath, a little scene,   164
To monarchize, be feared, and kill with looks,   165
Infusing him with self and vain conceit,   166

168 **and humored thus** and Death, having amused himself at the King's expense, having led the King on in this humor

171 **Cover your heads** Replace your hats (which have been removed out of respect for the King)

176 **Subjected** Made subject to grief, want, etc. (With pun on "being treated like a subject.")

179 **But . . . wail** but promptly anticipate and thus prevent the courses that result in lamentation.

180–1 **To fear . . . foe** i.e., To be afraid of the foe is merely a weakness that, by oppressing your own resolve, gives advantage to the foe

183 **Fear . . . fight** i.e., If you fear, you are sure to be slain, and no worse fate can come to you if you fight

184–5 **fight . . . breath** to die fighting is to conquer death in the very act of dying, whereas to die fearfully pays to death the tribute of servility.

186 **power** army (as also in line 192).   **of** about, or from

187 **learn . . . limb** i.e., discover how to make a partial force substitute for a complete one.

189 **change** exchange.   **for . . . doom** i.e., in order to settle our fates, which of us is to die now.

190 **This ague . . . overblown** This paroxysm of shivering in fear has blown over

191 **our own** i.e., my own kingdom.

194 **complexion** appearance

As if this flesh which walls about our life
Were brass impregnable; and humored thus,   168
Comes at the last and with a little pin
Bores through his castle wall, and—farewell, king!
Cover your heads, and mock not flesh and blood   171
With solemn reverence. Throw away respect,
Tradition, form, and ceremonious duty,
For you have but mistook me all this while.
I live with bread like you, feel want,
Taste grief, need friends. Subjected thus,   176
How can you say to me I am a king?

CARLISLE
My lord, wise men ne'er sit and wail their woes,
But presently prevent the ways to wail.   179
To fear the foe, since fear oppresseth strength,   180
Gives in your weakness strength unto your foe,   181
And so your follies fight against yourself.
Fear, and be slain. No worse can come to fight;   183
And fight and die is death destroying death,   184
Where fearing dying pays death servile breath.   185

AUMERLE
My father hath a power. Inquire of him,   186
And learn to make a body of a limb.   187

KING RICHARD
Thou chid'st me well. Proud Bolingbroke, I come
To change blows with thee for our day of doom.   189
This ague fit of fear is overblown;   190
An easy task it is to win our own.   191
Say, Scroop, where lies our uncle with his power?
Speak sweetly, man, although thy looks be sour.

SCROOP
Men judge by the complexion of the sky   194
    The state and inclination of the day.
So may you by my dull and heavy eye;
    My tongue hath but a heavier tale to say.

198 **by small and small** little by little

202–3 **And . . . party** and all your men of rank in southern England are also in arms on Bolingbroke's side.

204 **Beshrew** Confound. (Literally, *curse*.)   **forth** out

209 **Flint Castle** (Near Chester.)

212 **ear** plow

215 **double wrong** i.e., in deceiving me and in leading me into false hope once again

3.3 *Location: Wales. Before Flint Castle.*

1 **intelligence** information

I play the torturer, by small and small   198
To lengthen out the worst that must be spoken:
Your uncle York is joined with Bolingbroke,
And all your northern castles yielded up,
And all your southern gentlemen in arms   202
Upon his party.

KING RICHARD   Thou hast said enough.   203
 [*To Aumerle*] Beshrew thee, cousin, which didst lead
  me forth   204
Of that sweet way I was in to despair.
What say you now? What comfort have we now?
By heaven, I'll hate him everlastingly
That bids me be of comfort any more.
Go to Flint Castle. There I'll pine away;   209
A king, woe's slave, shall kingly woe obey.
That power I have, discharge, and let them go
To ear the land that hath some hope to grow,   212
For I have none. Let no man speak again
To alter this, for counsel is but vain.

AUMERLE
 My liege, one word.

KING RICHARD   He does me double wrong   215
 That wounds me with the flatteries of his tongue.
Discharge my followers. Let them hence away,
From Richard's night to Bolingbroke's fair day.

         [*Exeunt.*]

[3.3] ⮑ *Enter [with drum and colors] Bolingbroke, York,*
   Northumberland, [attendants, and forces].

BOLINGBROKE
 So that by this intelligence we learn   1
 The Welshmen are dispersed, and Salisbury
 Is gone to meet the King, who lately landed
 With some few private friends upon this coast.

7 **beseem** be appropriate for, be seemly behavior in

13 **to** as to

14 **taking so the head** i.e., (1) presumptuously omitting thus his title (2) being headstrong

17 **mistake** fail to perceive that. (Plays on Bolingbroke's use of *mistake*, just as York has punned on *brief* and *head*.)

25 **lies** resides

NORTHUMBERLAND

The news is very fair and good, my lord:
Richard not far from hence hath hid his head.

YORK

It would beseem the Lord Northumberland   7
To say "King Richard." Alack the heavy day
When such a sacred king should hide his head!

NORTHUMBERLAND

Your Grace mistakes. Only to be brief
Left I his title out.

YORK   The time hath been,
Would you have been so brief with him, he would
Have been so brief with you to shorten you,   13
For taking so the head, your whole head's length.   14

BOLINGBROKE

Mistake not, uncle, further than you should.

YORK

Take not, good cousin, further than you should,
Lest you mistake the heavens are over our heads.   17

BOLINGBROKE

I know it, uncle, and oppose not myself
Against their will. But who comes here?

          Enter Percy.

Welcome, Harry. What, will not this castle yield?

PERCY

The castle royally is manned, my lord,
Against thy entrance.

BOLINGBROKE

Royally? Why, it contains no king?

PERCY   Yes, my good lord,
It doth contain a king. King Richard lies   25
Within the limits of yon lime and stone,
And with him are the Lord Aumerle, Lord Salisbury,

30 **belike** probably

32 **rude ribs** i.e., rugged walls

33 **brazen** (1) brass (2) bold.   **breath of parley** i.e., call
for a conference

34 **his ruined ears** i.e., its (the castle's) ancient and battered
loopholes

40 **my banishment repealed** the revocation of my banishment

41 **lands restored again** the restoration of my lands

42 **advantage of my power** superiority of my army

46 **is** is that

48 **stooping duty** submissive kneeling

52 **tottered** in tottering condition, or dilapidated

53 **fair appointments** handsome show of military pre-
paredness

56 **fire and water** i.e., lightning and rain

Sir Stephen Scroop, besides a clergyman
Of holy reverence—who, I cannot learn.

NORTHUMBERLAND
    Oh, belike it is the Bishop of Carlisle.   30

BOLINGBROKE [*to Northumberland*]   Noble lord,
    Go to the rude ribs of that ancient castle;   32
    Through brazen trumpet send the breath of parley   33
    Into his ruined ears, and thus deliver: 34
    Henry Bolingbroke
    On both his knees doth kiss King Richard's hand
    And sends allegiance and true faith of heart
    To his most royal person, hither come
    Even at his feet to lay my arms and power,
    Provided that my banishment repealed   40
    And lands restored again be freely granted.   41
    If not, I'll use the advantage of my power,   42
    And lay the summer's dust with showers of blood
    Rained from the wounds of slaughtered Englishmen—
    The which how far off from the mind of Bolingbroke
    It is such crimson tempest should bedrench   46
    The fresh green lap of fair King Richard's land,
    My stooping duty tenderly shall show.   48
    Go, signify as much while here we march
    Upon the grassy carpet of this plain.
       [*Northumberland and attendants advance to the castle.*]
    Let's march without the noise of threat'ning drum,
    That from this castle's tottered battlements   52
    Our fair appointments may be well perused.   53
    Methinks King Richard and myself should meet
    With no less terror than the elements
    Of fire and water, when their thund'ring shock   56
    At meeting tears the cloudy cheeks of heaven.
    Be he the fire, I'll be the yielding water;

59–60 **whilst . . . waters** while I moisten the earth with my tears

61.2 *parley* trumpet summons to a negotiation

61.4 *on the walls* i.e., in the gallery of the tiring-house, above, to the rear of the stage

63 **blushing** i.e., turning red with anger

65 **he** i.e., the sun. **envious** hostile

67 **occident** west.

68 **Yet** Still, or nevertheless. **he** i.e., King Richard

69 **lightens forth** flashes out, like lightning

73 **watch** wait for

76 **awful** reverential, full of awe

77 **hand** signature

79 **no . . . bone** no human hand

81 **Unless he do profane** without committing sacrilege

83 **Have . . . us** have imperiled their souls by turning traitor to me

84 **And** and that

85 **know** know that

The rage be his, whilst on the earth I rain   59
My waters—on the earth, and not on him.   60
March on, and mark King Richard how he looks.   61

> [*Bolingbroke's forces march about the stage.*] *The*
> *trumpets sound* [*a parley without and answer*
> *within, then a flourish. King*] *Richard appeareth*
> *on the walls* [*with the Bishop of Carlisle, Aumerle,*
> *Scroop, and Salisbury*].

See, see, King Richard doth himself appear,
As doth the blushing discontented sun   63
From out the fiery portal of the east
When he perceives the envious clouds are bent   65
To dim his glory and to stain the track
Of his bright passage to the occident.   67

YORK
Yet looks he like a king. Behold, his eye,   68
As bright as is the eagle's, lightens forth   69
Controlling majesty. Alack, alack, for woe,
That any harm should stain so fair a show!

KING RICHARD [*to Northumberland*]
We are amazed; and thus long have we stood
To watch the fearful bending of thy knee,   73
Because we thought ourself thy lawful king.
And if we be, how dare thy joints forget
To pay their awful duty to our presence?   76
If we be not, show us the hand of God   77
That hath dismissed us from our stewardship;
For well we know, no hand of blood and bone   79
Can grip the sacred handle of our scepter,
Unless he do profane, steal, or usurp.   81
And though you think that all, as you have done,
Have torn their souls by turning them from us,   83
And we are barren and bereft of friends,   84
Yet know, my master, God omnipotent,   85

89 **That** of you that.   **vassal** subject

90 **threat** threaten

93–4 **open . . . testament** initiate a bloodstained legacy. (Blood was often said to be purple.)

96–7 **Ten . . . face** the bloody heads of 10,000 young men (the flower of England) will disfigure the blossoming face of our country

98 **maid-pale** i.e., pale like the complexion of a young English maid

102 **civil** used in civil strife.   **uncivil** barbarous, violent

108 **head** source

112 **scope** purpose, aim

113 **lineal royalties** hereditary rights as one of royal blood

114 **Enfranchisement** freedom (from banishment)

115 **party** part

116 **commend** give over

117 **barbèd** armored

Is mustering in his clouds on our behalf
Armies of pestilence; and they shall strike
Your children yet unborn and unbegot,
That lift your vassal hands against my head   89
And threat the glory of my precious crown.   90
Tell Bolingbroke—for yon methinks he stands—
That every stride he makes upon my land
Is dangerous treason. He is come to open   93
The purple testament of bleeding war;   94
But ere the crown he looks for live in peace,
Ten thousand bloody crowns of mothers' sons   96
Shall ill become the flower of England's face,   97
Change the complexion of her maid-pale peace   98
To scarlet indignation, and bedew
Her pastures' grass with faithful English blood.

NORTHUMBERLAND
The King of heaven forbid our lord the King
Should so with civil and uncivil arms   102
Be rushed upon! Thy thrice-noble cousin
Harry Bolingbroke doth humbly kiss thy hand;
And by the honorable tomb he swears
That stands upon your royal grandsire's bones,
And by the royalties of both your bloods,
Currents that spring from one most gracious head,   108
And by the buried hand of warlike Gaunt,
And by the worth and honor of himself,
Comprising all that may be sworn or said,
His coming hither hath no further scope   112
Than for his lineal royalties, and to beg   113
Enfranchisement immediate on his knees;   114
Which on thy royal party granted once,   115
His glittering arms he will commend to rust,   116
His barbèd steeds to stables, and his heart   117
To faithful service of Your Majesty.

121 **returns** answers
124 **accomplished** fulfilled
126 **commends** regards.
128 **poorly** abject.   **fair** courteously.
136 **sooth** cajolery, flattery.
140 **scope** freedom, space
141 **scope** capacity, opportunity

This swears he, as he is a prince and just,
And as I am a gentleman I credit him.

KING RICHARD
   Northumberland, say thus the King returns: 121
   His noble cousin is right welcome hither,
   And all the number of his fair demands
   Shall be accomplished without contradiction. 124
   With all the gracious utterance thou hast
   Speak to his gentle hearing kind commends. 126
       [Northumberland and attendants retire to Bolingbroke
                   and York.]

   [To Aumerle] We do debase ourself, cousin, do we not,
   To look so poorly and to speak so fair? 128
   Shall we call back Northumberland, and send
   Defiance to the traitor, and so die?

AUMERLE
   No, good my lord. Let's fight with gentle words
   Till time lend friends, and friends their helpful swords.

KING RICHARD
   Oh, God, oh, God, that e'er this tongue of mine,
   That laid the sentence of dread banishment
   On yon proud man, should take it off again
   With words of sooth! Oh, that I were as great 136
   As is my grief, or lesser than my name!
   Or that I could forget what I have been,
   Or not remember what I must be now!
   Swell'st thou, proud heart? I'll give thee scope to beat, 140
   Since foes have scope to beat both thee and me. 141
          [Northumberland returns to the castle walls.]

AUMERLE
   Northumberland comes back from Bolingbroke.

KING RICHARD
   What must the King do now? Must he submit?
   The King shall do it. Must he be deposed?
   The King shall be contented. Must he lose

147 **set of beads** rosary

149 **almsman's gown** plain attire of one who lives on alms or charity

150 **figured** ornamented, embossed

151 **palmer's** pilgrim's

156 **trade** passage

159 **buried once** once I am buried

162 **Our . . . corn** our sighs and tears will beat down the summer grain fields

163 **revolting** rebelling

164 **play the wantons** sport, frolic

165 **match** game, contest

166 **still** continually

167 **fretted us** eaten away for us, worn. (With a play on "complained.")

169 **digged** who dug

175 **a leg** an obeisance

176 **base court** outer or lower court of a castle

177 **may it please you** if you please

178 **glistering** glistening, glittering.   **Phäethon** son of the sun god, whose chariot he attempted to steer across the sky; unable to control the horses of the sun, he was hurled from the chariot by Jupiter

The name of king? I' God's name, let it go.
I'll give my jewels for a set of beads,   147
My gorgeous palace for a hermitage,
My gay apparel for an almsman's gown,   149
My figured goblets for a dish of wood,   150
My scepter for a palmer's walking-staff,   151
My subjects for a pair of carvèd saints,
And my large kingdom for a little grave,
A little, little grave, an obscure grave;
Or I'll be buried in the King's highway,
Some way of common trade, where subjects' feet   156
May hourly trample on their sovereign's head;
For on my heart they tread now whilst I live,
And, buried once, why not upon my head?   159
Aumerle, thou weep'st, my tenderhearted cousin.
We'll make foul weather with despisèd tears;
Our sighs and they shall lodge the summer corn   162
And make a dearth in this revolting land.   163
Or shall we play the wantons with our woes   164
And make some pretty match with shedding tears?   165
As thus, to drop them still upon one place,   166
Till they have fretted us a pair of graves   167
Within the earth; and, therein laid, there lies
Two kinsmen digged their graves with weeping eyes.   169
Would not this ill do well? Well, well, I see
I talk but idly, and you laugh at me.—
Most mighty prince, my lord Northumberland,
What says King Bolingbroke? Will His Majesty
Give Richard leave to live till Richard die?
You make a leg, and Bolingbroke says ay.   175

NORTHUMBERLAND
My lord, in the base court he doth attend   176
To speak with you, may it please you to come down.   177

KING RICHARD
Down, down I come, like glistering Phaëthon,   178

179 **Wanting . . . jades** lacking the skill in horsemanship
     to control unruly nags.

181 **do them grace** (1) bow to them (2) treat them gra-
     ciously.

185 **fondly** foolishly.   **frantic** mad

187 **apart** aside

188 **fair duty** respect

190–91 **debase . . . base** (Continues the wordplay on *base*
     in line 180.)

192 **Me rather had** I had rather

198 **mine** i.e., my loved lord (changing Richard's meaning
     of *yours* in the previous line).   **redoubted** dread

Wanting the manage of unruly jades.   179
In the base court? Base court, where kings grow base,
To come at traitors' calls and do them grace.   181
In the base court? Come down? Down, court! Down,
    king!
For night owls shriek where mounting larks should
    sing.   [*Exeunt from above.*]

[*Northumberland rejoins Bolingbroke.*]

BOLINGBROKE
What says His Majesty?

NORTHUMBERLAND   Sorrow and grief of heart
Makes him speak fondly, like a frantic man.   185
Yet he is come.

[*Enter King Richard and his attendants below.*]

BOLINGBROKE   Stand all apart,   187
And show fair duty to His Majesty.   *He kneels down.*   188
My gracious lord!

KING RICHARD
Fair cousin, you debase your princely knee   190
To make the base earth proud with kissing it.   191
Me rather had my heart might feel your love   192
Than my unpleased eye see your courtesy.
Up, cousin, up. Your heart is up, I know,
Thus high at least [*touching his crown*], although your
    knee be low.

BOLINGBROKE [*rising*]
My gracious lord, I come but for mine own.

KING RICHARD
Your own is yours, and I am yours, and all.

BOLINGBROKE
So far be mine, my most redoubted lord,   198
As my true service shall deserve your love.

203 **want their remedies** lack remedies for what caused
   them.

204 **too young** (Historically Richard and Bolingbroke were
   both thirty-three.)

3.4 *Location: The Duke of York's garden.*

3 **bowls** lawn bowling. (A common Elizabethan game.)

4 **rubs** impediments (in the game of bowls)

5 **against the bias** i.e., contrary, athwart. (Literally, not
   following the naturally curved path of a bowl, which was
   weighted on one side.)

7 **measure** a stately slow dance

8 **measure** moderation

KING RICHARD
    Well you deserve. They well deserve to have
    That know the strong'st and surest way to get.
    [*To York, who weeps*] Uncle, give me your hands. Nay,
        dry your eyes;
    Tears show their love, but want their remedies.   203
    [*To Bolingbroke*] Cousin, I am too young to be your
        father,   204
    Though you are old enough to be my heir.
    What you will have, I'll give, and willing too,
    For do we must what force will have us do.
    Set on towards London, cousin, is it so?

BOLINGBROKE
    Yea, my good lord.

KING RICHARD   Then I must not say no.
                                        [*Flourish. Exeunt.*]

[3.4] ✢ *Enter the Queen with [two Ladies,] her attendants.*

QUEEN
    What sport shall we devise here in this garden,
    To drive away the heavy thought of care?

LADY   Madam, we'll play at bowls.   3

QUEEN
    'Twill make me think the world is full of rubs,   4
    And that my fortune runs against the bias.   5

LADY   Madam, we'll dance.

QUEEN
    My legs can keep no measure in delight   7
    When my poor heart no measure keeps in grief.   8
    Therefore, no dancing, girl; some other sport.

LADY   Madam, we'll tell tales.

QUEEN
    Of sorrow or of joy?

13 **wanting** lacking

14 **remember** remind

18 **boots** helps

20 **wouldst thou** if you would

22 **would . . . good** i.e., if weeping would make me any less unhappy

23 **never borrow** never need to borrow

26 **My . . . pins** i.e., I'd bet my immeasurable grief against the merest trifle

27 **state** statecraft, politics

28 **Against . . . with woe** when change is imminent; sad times are heralded by gloomy predictions.

31 **prodigal** excessive

LADY   Of either, madam.

QUEEN   Of neither, girl;
    For if of joy, being altogether wanting,   13
    It doth remember me the more of sorrow;   14
    Or if of grief, being altogether had,
    It adds more sorrow to my want of joy.
    For what I have I need not to repeat,
    And what I want it boots not to complain.   18

LADY
    Madam, I'll sing.

QUEEN   'Tis well that thou hast cause,
    But thou shouldst please me better wouldst thou
        weep.   20

LADY
    I could weep, madam, would it do you good.

QUEEN
    And I could sing, would weeping do me good,   22
    And never borrow any tear of thee.   23

        Enter Gardeners [a Master and two Men].

    But stay, here come the gardeners.
    Let's step into the shadow of these trees.
    My wretchedness unto a row of pins,   26
    They will talk of state, for everyone doth so   27
    Against a change; woe is forerun with woe.   28
                    [The Queen and Ladies stand apart.]

GARDENER *[to one Man]*
    Go bind thou up young dangling apricots
    Which, like unruly children, make their sire
    Stoop with oppression of their prodigal weight.   31
    Give some supportance to the bending twigs.
    [To the other] Go thou, and like an executioner
    Cut off the heads of too-fast-growing sprays
    That look too lofty in our commonwealth.

36 **even** equal

38 **noisome** harmful

40 **pale** enclosure, enclosed garden

42 **firm** stable

46 **knots** flower beds laid out in intricate designs

48 **suffered** allowed

49 **fall of leaf** i.e., autumn.

51 **in eating him** i.e., while they were really eating his sustenance

56 **dressed** put in order

57 **at . . . year** in the appropriate season

59 **overproud in** swollen with

64 **bearing** fruit-bearing

All must be even in our government.   36
You thus employed, I will go root away
The noisome weeds which without profit suck   38
The soil's fertility from wholesome flowers.

MAN

Why should we in the compass of a pale   40
Keep law and form and due proportion,
Showing as in a model our firm estate,   42
When our sea-wallèd garden, the whole land,
Is full of weeds, her fairest flowers choked up,
Her fruit trees all unpruned, her hedges ruined,
Her knots disordered, and her wholesome herbs   46
Swarming with caterpillars?

GARDENER   Hold thy peace.
He that hath suffered this disordered spring   48
Hath now himself met with the fall of leaf.   49
The weeds which his broad-spreading leaves did
    shelter,
That seemed in eating him to hold him up,   51
Are plucked up root and all by Bolingbroke:
I mean the Earl of Wiltshire, Bushy, Green.

MAN

What, are they dead?

GARDENER   They are; and Bolingbroke
Hath seized the wasteful King. Oh, what pity is it
That he had not so trimmed and dressed his land   56
As we this garden! We at time of year   57
Do wound the bark, the skin of our fruit trees,
Lest being overproud in sap and blood   59
With too much riches it confound itself;
Had he done so to great and growing men,
They might have lived to bear and he to taste
Their fruits of duty. Superfluous branches
We lop away, that bearing boughs may live;   64

65 **crown** (1) royal crown (2) crown of a tree

68 **Depressed** Brought low

69 **'Tis doubt** there is fear

71 **pressed to death** (Allusion to the *peine forte et dure*, in-flicted by pressure of heavy weights upon the chests of indicted persons who refused to plead and remained silent.)

72 **old Adam** (In his role as the first gardener.)

73 **dress** cultivate

75 **suggested** tempted

79 **Divine** prophesy

90 **Post** Hasten. (See the note at 1.1.56.)

93 **embassage** message.   **belong to** concern

Had he done so, himself had borne the crown   65
Which waste of idle hours hath quite thrown down.

MAN
What, think you the King shall be deposed?

GARDENER
Depressed he is already, and deposed   68
'Tis doubt he will be. Letters came last night   69
To a dear friend of the good Duke of York's,
That tell black tidings.

QUEEN [coming forward]   Oh, I am pressed to death   71
Through want of speaking! Thou, old Adam's likeness,   72
Set to dress this garden, how dares   73
Thy harsh rude tongue sound this unpleasing news?
What Eve, what serpent, hath suggested thee   75
To make a second fall of cursèd man?
Why dost thou say King Richard is deposed?
Dar'st thou, thou little better thing than earth,
Divine his downfall? Say where, when, and how   79
Cam'st thou by this ill tidings? Speak, thou wretch.

GARDENER
Pardon me, madam. Little joy have I
To breathe this news, yet what I say is true.
King Richard, he is in the mighty hold
Of Bolingbroke. Their fortunes both are weighed:
In your lord's scale is nothing but himself
And some few vanities that make him light;
But in the balance of great Bolingbroke,
Besides himself, are all the English peers,
And with that odds he weighs King Richard down.
Post you to London and you will find it so;   90
I speak no more than everyone doth know.

QUEEN
Nimble mischance, that art so light of foot,
Doth not thy embassage belong to me,   93
And am I last that knows it? Oh, thou thinkest

96 **Thy sorrow** the sorrow that you (mischance) report

99 **triumph** triumphal procession.   **Bolingbroke** (The original spelling, "Bullingbrooke," indicates the rhyme with *look* in the previous line, pronounced something like "bruke" and "luke.")

102 **So that** Provided that

104 **fall** let fall

105 **rue** "herb of grace," a plant symbolical of repentance, ruth, or sorrow for another's misery

106 **ruth** pity

4.1 *Location: Westminster Hall.*

4 **Who . . . King** who prevailed upon the King to have the murder performed

5 **office** function.   **timeless** untimely

To serve me last, that I may longest keep
Thy sorrow in my breast.—Come, ladies, go   96
To meet at London London's king in woe.
What, was I born to this, that my sad look
Should grace the triumph of great Bolingbroke?   99
Gard'ner, for telling me these news of woe,
Pray God the plants thou graft'st may never grow.

Exit [with Ladies].

GARDENER
Poor queen! So that thy state might be no worse,   102
I would my skill were subject to thy curse.
Here did she fall a tear; here in this place   104
I'll set a bank of rue, sour herb of grace.   105
Rue even for ruth here shortly shall be seen,   106
In the remembrance of a weeping queen.   *Exeunt.*

[4.1] ❧ *Enter Bolingbroke with the Lords [Aumerle,*
Northumberland, Harry Percy, Fitzwater, Surrey,
the Bishop of Carlisle, the Abbot of Westminster,
and another Lord, Herald, officers] to Parliament.
[The throne is provided on stage.]

BOLINGBROKE
Call forth Bagot.

Enter [officers with] Bagot.

Now, Bagot, freely speak thy mind,
What thou dost know of noble Gloucester's death,
Who wrought it with the King, and who performed   4
The bloody office of his timeless end.   5

BAGOT
Then set before my face the Lord Aumerle.

BOLINGBROKE [*to Aumerle*]
Cousin, stand forth, and look upon that man.

[Aumerle comes forward.]

 9 **unsay** deny, take back.   **delivered** reported.

10 **dead** (1) deadly (2) dark, silent

11 **of length** long

12 **restful** i.e., untroubled by Gloucester

14 **that very time** (An inconsistency; Gloucester's death occurred before Bolingbroke left England.)

17 **Than . . . return** than have Bolingbroke return

18 **withal** in addition

22 **stars** i.e., fortune, rank

23 **On . . . chastisement** as to challenge him as my equal.

25 **attainder** dishonoring accusation

25.1 *gage* usually a glove or a gauntlet (a mailed or armored glove), as at 1.1.69ff.

26 **manual . . . death** death warrant sealed by my hand

32 **one** i.e., Bolingbroke.   **best** highest in rank

34 **stand on sympathy** i.e., insists on correspondence of rank in your opponent

35 **in gage** engaged

37 **vauntingly** boastfully

BAGOT

My lord Aumerle, I know your daring tongue
Scorns to unsay what once it hath delivered.　9
In that dead time when Gloucester's death was plotted,　10
I heard you say, "Is not my arm of length,　11
That reacheth from the restful English court　12
As far as Calais, to mine uncle's head?"
Amongst much other talk that very time　14
I heard you say that you had rather refuse
The offer of an hundred thousand crowns
Than Bolingbroke's return to England—　17
Adding withal how blest this land would be　18
In this your cousin's death.

AUMERLE　Princes and noble lords,
What answer shall I make to this base man?
Shall I so much dishonor my fair stars　22
On equal terms to give him chastisement?　23
Either I must, or have mine honor soiled
With the attainder of his slanderous lips.　25

[He throws down his gage.]

There is my gage, the manual seal of death,　26
That marks thee out for hell. I say thou liest,
And will maintain what thou hast said is false
In thy heart-blood, though being all too base
To stain the temper of my knightly sword.

BOLINGBROKE

Bagot, forbear. Thou shalt not take it up.

AUMERLE　Bolingbroke
Excepting one, I would he were the best　highest in rank　32
In all this presence that hath moved me so.

FITZWATER *[throwing down a gage]*

If that thy valor stand on sympathy,　34
There is my gage, Aumerle, in gage to thine.　35
By that fair sun which shows me where thou stand'st,
I heard thee say, and vauntingly thou spak'st it,　37

40 **turn** turn back

46 **appeal** accusation. (As also in line 80.)   **all unjust** totally false

48–9 **to . . . breathing** to the point of death.

50 **An if** If

51 **more** any more, ever again

53 **I . . . like** I burden the ground in the same way

54 **lies** accusations of lying

56 **sun to sun** sunrise to sunset.   **honor's pawn** pledge of honor. (Also in line 71.)

57 **Engage . . . trial** take it up as a pledge to combat

58 **Who . . . else?** Who else puts up stakes against me or challenges me to a game?   **throw** (1) throw dice (2) throw down gages

That thou wert cause of noble Gloucester's death.
If thou deny'st it twenty times, thou liest,
And I will turn thy falsehood to thy heart,   40
Where it was forgèd, with my rapier's point.

AUMERLE [*taking up the gage*]
Thou dar'st not, coward, live to see that day.

FITZWATER
Now, by my soul, I would it were this hour.

AUMERLE
Fitzwater, thou art damned to hell for this.

PERCY   *accusation*
Aumerle, thou liest. His honor is as true
In this appeal as thou art all unjust;   46
And that thou art so, there I throw my gage

[*throwing down a gage*]

To prove it on thee to the extremest point   48
Of mortal breathing. Seize it if thou dar'st.   49

AUMERLE [*taking up the gage*]
An if I do not, may my hands rot off   50
And never brandish more revengeful steel   51
Over the glittering helmet of my foe!

ANOTHER LORD [*throwing down a gage*]
I task the earth to the like, forsworn Aumerle,   53
And spur thee on with full as many lies   54
As may be holloed in thy treacherous ear
From sun to sun. There is my honor's pawn;   56
Engage it to the trial, if thou darest.   57

AUMERLE [*taking up the gage*]
Who sets me else? By heaven, I'll throw at all!   58
I have a thousand spirits in one breast
To answer twenty thousand such as you.

SURREY
My lord Fitzwater, I do remember well
The very time Aumerle and you did talk.

63 **in presence** present
68 **it** i.e., my sword
73 **fondly** foolishly.   **forward** willing
75 **in a wilderness** i.e., where fighting might go on un-
interrupted to the death
79 **in . . . world** i.e., under the new king
80 **appeal** accusation.
86 **repealed** recalled from exile.   **try** test
87 **under gage** as challenges

FITZWATER
　　'Tis very true. You were in presence then,   63
　　And you can witness with me this is true.

SURREY　　As false, by heaven, as heaven itself is true.

FITZWATER
　　Surrey, thou liest.

SURREY　　　　　　Dishonorable boy!
　　That lie shall lie so heavy on my sword
　　That it shall render vengeance and revenge,   68
　　Till thou the lie-giver and that lie do lie
　　In earth as quiet as thy father's skull.
　　In proof whereof, there is my honor's pawn.

　　　　　　　　　　　　[*He throws down a gage.*]

　　Engage it to the trial if thou dar'st.

FITZWATER [*taking up the gage*]
　　How fondly dost thou spur a forward horse!   73
　　If I dare eat, or drink, or breathe, or live,
　　I dare meet Surrey in a wilderness   75
　　And spit upon him whilst I say he lies,
　　And lies, and lies. There is my bond of faith,
　　To tie thee to my strong correction.

　　　　　　　　　　　　[*He throws down a gage.*]

　　As I intend to thrive in this new world,   79
　　Aumerle is guilty of my true appeal.   80
　　Besides, I heard the banished Norfolk say
　　That thou, Aumerle, didst send two of thy men
　　To execute the noble Duke at Calais.

AUMERLE　　*draws a parallel with Mowbray*
　　Some honest Christian trust me with a gage.

　　　　　　[*He borrows a gage and throws it down.*]

　　That Norfolk lies, here do I throw down this,
　　If he may be repealed, to try his honor.   86

BOLINGBROKE
　　These differences shall all rest under gage   87

95 **Streaming** flying

97 **toiled** wearied

104–5 **bosom . . . Abraham** i.e., heaven. (See Luke 16:22.)

105 **Lords appellants** Lords who appear as formal accusers

107.1 *Enter York* (Probably Richard's scepter, etc., are brought in at line 162, but York here invites Bolingbroke to ascend the throne with the surrendered scepter, and so perhaps the regalia are brought on here.)

116 **Worst** Least in rank

Till Norfolk be repealed. Repealed he shall be,
And, though mine enemy, restored again
To all his lands and seigniories. When he is returned,
Against Aumerle we will enforce his trial.

CARLISLE
That honorable day shall never be seen.
Many a time hath banished Norfolk fought
For Jesu Christ in glorious Christian field,
Streaming the ensign of the Christian cross   95
Against black pagans, Turks, and Saracens;
And, toiled with works of war, retired himself   97
To Italy, and there at Venice gave
His body to that pleasant country's earth
And his pure soul unto his captain, Christ,
Under whose colors he had fought so long.

Holished:
Mowbray dies
in Venice

maintain
some sense
of dignity

BOLINGBROKE   Why, Bishop, is Norfolk dead?

CARLISLE   As surely as I live, my lord.

BOLINGBROKE
Sweet peace conduct his sweet soul to the bosom   104
Of good old Abraham! Lords appellants,   105
Your differences shall all rest under gage
Till we assign you to your days of trial.   107

Lord who
appear as
formal accusers

        Enter York.

YORK
Great Duke of Lancaster, I come to thee
From plume-plucked Richard, who with willing soul
Adopts thee heir, and his high scepter yields
To the possession of thy royal hand.
Ascend his throne, descending now from him,
And long live Henry, fourth of that name!

BOLINGBROKE
In God's name, I'll ascend the regal throne.

CARLISLE   Marry, God forbid!
Worst in this royal presence may I speak,   116

117 **best beseeming me** i.e., most befitting to me as a clergyman

120 **noblesse** nobleness

121 **Learn him forbearance** teach him to forbear

124 **judged . . . by** condemned unless they are present

125 **apparent** manifest

126 **figure** image

130 **forefend** forbid

131 **souls refined** civilized people

132 **obscene** odious, repulsive

135 **My . . . Hereford** (Carlisle refuses to refer to
Bolingbroke as king or even as Duke of Lancaster,
since he lost the latter title at the time of his banishment.)

142 **Shall . . . confound** will destroy kinsmen by means of
kinsmen and fellow countrymen by means of fellow
countrymen

145 **Golgotha** Calvary, the hill outside of Jerusalem called
"the place of dead men's skulls" (see Mark 15:22 and
John 19:17) where Jesus was crucified

146 **this house . . . this house** i.e., Lancaster against York.
(See Mark 3:25.)

Yet best beseeming me to speak the truth.   117
Would God that any in this noble presence
Were enough noble to be upright judge
Of noble Richard! Then true noblesse would   120
Learn him forbearance from so foul a wrong.   121
What subject can give sentence on his king?
And who sits here that is not Richard's subject?
Thieves are not judged but they are by to hear,   124
Although apparent guilt be seen in them;   125
And shall the figure of God's majesty,   126
His captain, steward, deputy elect,
Anointed, crownèd, planted many years,
Be judged by subject and inferior breath,
And he himself not present? Oh, forefend it God   130
That in a Christian climate souls refined   131
Should show so heinous, black, obscene a deed!   132
I speak to subjects, and a subject speaks,
Stirred up by God thus boldly for his king.
My lord of Hereford here, whom you call king,   135
Is a foul traitor to proud Hereford's king.
And if you crown him, let me prophesy:
The blood of English shall manure the ground
And future ages groan for this foul act;
Peace shall go sleep with Turks and infidels,
And in this seat of peace tumultuous wars
Shall kin with kin and kind with kind confound;   142
Disorder, horror, fear, and mutiny
Shall here inhabit, and this land be called
The field of Golgotha and dead men's skulls.   145
Oh, if you raise this house against this house,   146
It will the woefullest division prove
That ever fell upon this cursèd earth.
Prevent it, resist it, let it not be so,
Lest child, child's children, cry against you woe!

152 **Of** on a charge of

155 **the commons' suit** request of the commons (i.e., that Richard be formally tried and the causes of his deposition made public. This line begins the abdication passage omitted in early quartos of the play.)

157 **surrender** i.e., surrender the crown, abdicate

158 **conduct** escort.

160 **sureties** persons who will guarantee your appearance. **your days of answer** the time when you must appear to stand trial.

161 **beholding** beholden, indebted

162 **little . . . hands** i.e., I did not expect this from you, thinking you were on our side.

169 **favors** (1) faces (2) support, good will

174 **priest and clerk** (In religious services, the clerk or assistant would say "Amen" to the priest's prayers.)

NORTHUMBERLAND
>Well have you argued, sir, and for your pains
>Of capital treason we arrest you here.—   152
>My lord of Westminster, be it your charge
>To keep him safely till his day of trial.

>>>*[Carlisle is taken into custody.]*

>May it please you, lords, to grant the commons' suit?   155

BOLINGBROKE
>Fetch hither Richard, that in common view
>He may surrender; so we shall proceed   157
>Without suspicion.

YORK   I will be his conduct.   *Exit.*   158

BOLINGBROKE
>Lords, you that here are under our arrest,
>Procure your sureties for your days of answer.   160
>Little are we beholding to your love,   161
>And little looked for at your helping hands.   162

>>*Enter Richard and York [with Officers bearing
>>the crown and regalia].*

KING RICHARD
>Alack, why am I sent for to a king,
>Before I have shook off the regal thoughts
>Wherewith I reigned? I hardly yet have learned
>To insinuate, flatter, bow, and bend my knee.
>Give sorrow leave awhile to tutor me
>To this submission. Yet I well remember
>The favors of these men. Were they not mine?   169
>Did they not sometime cry, "All hail!" to me?
>So Judas did to Christ. But he, in twelve,
>Found truth in all but one; I, in twelve thousand, none.
>God save the King! Will no man say amen?
>Am I both priest and clerk? Well then, amen.   174
>God save the King, although I be not he;

186 **owes** owns, has.   **filling one another** (The raising
of the full bucket lowers the other to be filled in turn.)

196–200 **Your. . . stay** i.e., Your assuming the cares of office does not assuage my griefs. My grief is loss of
kingly responsibility, destroyed by a failure in diligence;
your concern is gaining of kingly responsibility, won
by zealous effort. The anxieties I transfer to you I also
keep for myself, despite my giving them to you; they
accompany the crown and yet still remain with me.

And yet, amen, if heaven do think him me.
To do what service am I sent for hither?

YORK
To do that office of thine own good will
Which tired majesty did make thee offer:
The resignation of thy state and crown
To Henry Bolingbroke.

KING RICHARD
Give me the crown. [*He takes the crown.*] Here, cousin,
    seize the crown.
Here, cousin,
On this side my hand, and on that side thine.
Now is this golden crown like a deep well
That owes two buckets, filling one another,   186
The emptier ever dancing in the air,
The other down, unseen, and full of water.
That bucket down and full of tears am I,
Drinking my griefs, whilst you mount up on high.

BOLINGBROKE
I thought you had been willing to resign.

KING RICHARD
My crown I am, but still my griefs are mine.
You may my glories and my state depose,
But not my griefs; still am I king of those.

BOLINGBROKE
Part of your cares you give me with your crown.

KING RICHARD
Your cares set up do not pluck my cares down.   196
My care is loss of care, by old care done;   197
Your care is gain of care, by new care won.   198
The cares I give I have, though given away;   199
They 'tend the crown, yet still with me they stay.   200

BOLINGBROKE
Are you contented to resign the crown?

202 **Ay** (1) Yes (2) I. (But, says Richard, I am nothing, and
     therefore "Ay" is "I" or "nothing," that is, "no.")

203 **no, no . . . thee** (Richard plays on the logic that a dou-
     ble negative equals a positive; with an aural pun on *no/
     know*.)

204 **undo** (1) divest (2) unmake

211 **release . . . oaths** release my subjects from their oaths
     of duty.

216 **are** that are

217 **Make** i.e., May God make.   **with nothing grieved**
     (1) grieved at nothing (2) grieved at having nothing

223 **read** i.e., read aloud

229 **ravel out** unravel

KING RICHARD

Ay, no; no, ay; for I must nothing be;   202
Therefore no, no, for I resign to thee.   203
Now mark me how I will undo myself: 204

                    [He yields his crown and scepter.]

I give this heavy weight from off my head
And this unwieldy scepter from my hand,
The pride of kingly sway from out my heart;
With mine own tears I wash away my balm,
With mine own hands I give away my crown,
With mine own tongue deny my sacred state,
With mine own breath release all duteous oaths.   211
All pomp and majesty I do forswear;
My manors, rents, revenues I forgo;
My acts, decrees, and statutes I deny.
God pardon all oaths that are broke to me!
God keep all vows unbroke are made to thee!   216
Make me, that nothing have, with nothing grieved,   217
And thou with all pleased, that hast all achieved!
Long mayst thou live in Richard's seat to sit,
And soon lie Richard in an earthy pit!
God save King Henry, unkinged Richard says,
And send him many years of sunshine days!—
What more remains?

NORTHUMBERLAND [*presenting a paper*]

                   No more but that you read   223
These accusations and these grievous crimes
Committed by your person and your followers
Against the state and profit of this land;
That, by confessing them, the souls of men
May deem that you are worthily deposed.

KING RICHARD

Must I do so? And must I ravel out   229
My weaved-up follies? Gentle Northumberland,
If thy offenses were upon record,

232 **troop** company

233 **read a lecture** give a public reading (as a warning)

237 **Marked . . . damned** (modifying *article* in line 234)

239 **bait** torment, harass (as in bearbaiting)

240 **wash your hands** (See Matthew 27:24. Richard persistently compares himself to Christ; see also 3.2.132; 4.1.171.)

242 **sour** bitter

244 **dispatch** conclude, be done.

247 **sort** gang

251 **pompous** stately, splendid

253 **state** high rank, stateliness

255 **haught** haughty

Would it not shame thee in so fair a troop   232
To read a lecture of them? If thou wouldst,   233
There shouldst thou find one heinous article
Containing the deposing of a king
And cracking the strong warrant of an oath,
Marked with a blot, damned in the book of heaven.   237
Nay, all of you that stand and look upon me,
Whilst that my wretchedness doth bait myself,   239
Though some of you, with Pilate, wash your hands,   240
Showing an outward pity, yet you Pilates
Have here delivered me to my sour cross,   242
And water cannot wash away your sin.

NORTHUMBERLAND
My lord, dispatch. Read o'er these articles.   244

KING RICHARD
Mine eyes are full of tears; I cannot see.
And yet salt water blinds them not so much
But they can see a sort of traitors here.   247
Nay, if I turn mine eyes upon myself,
I find myself a traitor with the rest;
For I have given here my soul's consent
T'undeck the pompous body of a king,   251
Made glory base and sovereignty a slave,
Proud majesty a subject, state a peasant.   253

NORTHUMBERLAND   My lord—

KING RICHARD
No lord of thine, thou haught insulting man,   255
Nor no man's lord. I have no name, no title,
No, not that name was given me at the font,
But 'tis usurped. Alack the heavy day,
That I have worn so many winters out
And know not now what name to call myself!
Oh, that I were a mockery king of snow,
Standing before the sun of Bolingbroke,
To melt myself away in water drops!

265 **An if** if.   **sterling** valid currency

266 **straight** immediately

268 **his** its

269 **some** i.e., someone

276.1 *glass* mirror.

281 **in prosperity** i.e., in my prosperity

282 **Was this face** (An echo of Christopher Marlowe's *Doctor Faustus*, 5.1, in which the protagonist addresses Helen of Troy.)

285 **wink** close the eyes, blink.

286 **faced** countenanced

287 **outfaced** stared down, discountenanced

Good king, great king, and yet not greatly good,
An if my word be sterling yet in England,   265
Let it command a mirror hither straight,   266
That it may show me what a face I have,
Since it is bankrupt of his majesty.   268

BOLINGBROKE
Go some of you and fetch a looking glass.   269
                                         [*Exit an Attendant.*]

NORTHUMBERLAND
Read o'er this paper while the glass doth come.

KING RICHARD
Fiend, thou torments me ere I come to hell!

BOLINGBROKE
Urge it no more, my lord Northumberland.

NORTHUMBERLAND
The commons will not then be satisfied.

KING RICHARD
They shall be satisfied. I'll read enough
When I do see the very book indeed
Where all my sins are writ, and that's myself.   276

      Enter one with a glass.

Give me that glass, and therein will I read.
                                  [*He takes the mirror.*]
No deeper wrinkles yet? Hath sorrow struck
So many blows upon this face of mine,
And made no deeper wounds? O flattering glass,
Like to my followers in prosperity,   281
Thou dost beguile me! Was this face the face   282
That every day under his household roof
Did keep ten thousand men? Was this the face
That, like the sun, did make beholders wink?   285
Is this the face which faced so many follies,   286
That was at last outfaced by Bolingbroke?   287

293 **shadow** outward show, or, overshadowing nature
294 **shadow** reflection (in the mirror)
297 **manners** forms, manifestations
298 **shadows to** shadowings forth or embodiments of
300 **There** i.e., In my soul
301 **that** you who
303 **boon** favor
309 **to** as

A brittle glory shineth in this face—
As brittle as the glory is the face,

                         [He throws down the mirror.]

For there it is, cracked in an hundred shivers.
Mark, silent king, the moral of this sport:
How soon my sorrow hath destroyed my face.

BOLINGBROKE
    The shadow of your sorrow hath destroyed   293
    The shadow of your face.

KING RICHARD   Say that again.   294
    The shadow of my sorrow? Ha! Let's see.
    'Tis very true, my grief lies all within;
    And these external manners of laments   297
    Are merely shadows to the unseen grief   298
    That swells with silence in the tortured soul.
    There lies the substance; and I thank thee, King,   300
    For thy great bounty, that not only giv'st   301
    Me cause to wail, but teachest me the way
    How to lament the cause. I'll beg one boon,   303
    And then be gone and trouble you no more.
    Shall I obtain it?

BOLINGBROKE   Name it, fair cousin.

KING RICHARD
    "Fair cousin"? I am greater than a king.
    For when I was a king, my flatterers
    Were then but subjects; being now a subject,
    I have a king here to my flatterer.   309
    Being so great, I have no need to beg.

BOLINGBROKE   Yet ask.

KING RICHARD   And shall I have?

BOLINGBROKE   You shall.

KING RICHARD   Then give me leave to go.

BOLINGBROKE   Whither?

317 **convey** escort
318 **Convey** Steal.
321.1 *Manent* They remain on stage
324 **Shall** who will
330 **To . . . intents** to conceal my plans
335 **shall** that shall

KING RICHARD

Whither you will, so I were from your sights.

BOLINGBROKE

Go some of you, convey him to the Tower.   317

KING RICHARD

Oh, good! "Convey"? Conveyers are you all,   318
That rise thus nimbly by a true king's fall.

[*Exeunt King Richard, some lords, and a guard.*]

BOLINGBROKE

On Wednesday next we solemnly set down
Our coronation. Lords, prepare yourselves.   321

Exeunt. Manent [*the Abbot of*] *Westminster,* [*the
Bishop of*] *Carlisle, Aumerle.*

ABBOT

A woeful pageant have we here beheld.

CARLISLE

The woe's to come, the children yet unborn
Shall feel this day as sharp to them as thorn.   324

AUMERLE

You holy clergymen, is there no plot
To rid the realm of this pernicious blot?

ABBOT   My lord,

Before I freely speak my mind herein,
You shall not only take the Sacrament
To bury mine intents, but also to effect   330
Whatever I shall happen to devise.
I see your brows are full of discontent,
Your hearts of sorrow, and your eyes of tears.
Come home with me to supper; I'll lay
A plot shall show us all a merry day.   *Exeunt.* 335

5.1 *Location: London. A street leading to the Tower.*

  2 **Julius . . . tower** (The Tower of London, ascribed by tradition to Julius Caesar, was built by William the Conqueror to hold the city in subordination.)   **ill-erected** erected for evil ends or with evil results

11 **thou . . . stand** i.e., you ruined majesty, pattern of fallen greatness like the desolate waste where Troy once stood

12 **map of honor** i.e., the mere outline of a once-glorious honor

13 **inn** residence, house

14 **hard-favored** unpleasant-looking

15 **is . . . guest** lodges in such a vulgar tavern (i.e., in Bolingbroke).

17 **To . . . sudden** to kill me quickly with grief.

22 **Hie** Hasten

23 **religious house** convent.

24 **new world's** heaven's

[5.1] ❧ *Enter the Queen with [Ladies,] her attendants.*

QUEEN

    This way the King will come. This is the way
    To Julius Caesar's ill-erected tower,   2
    To whose flint bosom my condemnèd lord
    Is doomed a prisoner by proud Bolingbroke.
    Here let us rest, if this rebellious earth
    Have any resting for her true king's queen.

        Enter Richard [and guard].

    But soft, but see, or rather do not see
    My fair rose wither. Yet look up, behold,
    That you in pity may dissolve to dew,
    And wash him fresh again with true-love tears.—
    Ah, thou, the model where old Troy did stand,   11
    Thou map of honor, thou King Richard's tomb,   12
    And not King Richard! Thou most beauteous inn,   13
    Why should hard-favored grief be lodged in thee   14
    When triumph is become an alehouse guest?   15

KING RICHARD

    Join not with grief, fair woman, do not so,
    To make my end too sudden. Learn, good soul,   17
    To think our former state a happy dream,
    From which awaked, the truth of what we are
    Shows us but this. I am sworn brother, sweet,
    To grim Necessity, and he and I
    Will keep a league till death. Hie thee to France,   22
    And cloister thee in some religious house.   23
    Our holy lives must win a new world's crown,   24
    Which our profane hours here have thrown down.

31 **To be** at being

34 **Which art** you who are

35 **king of beasts** (1) lion (2) ruler over beastly men

37 **sometimes** former

42 **Of . . . betid** of woe that happened ages ago

43 **quit their griefs** requite their tales of woe

46–7 **Forwhy . . . tongue** because even the inanimate and unfeeling firebrands will respond to the doleful tone of your affecting tale

49 **And . . . coal-black** and some of the brands will heap ashes on themselves like grieving mourners and turn black with charring as though dressing themselves in the black of mourning

52 **Pomfret** Pontefract Castle in Yorkshire

53 **order ta'en** arrangement made

QUEEN

    What, is my Richard both in shape and mind
    Transformed and weakened? Hath Bolingbroke
    Deposed thine intellect? Hath he been in thy heart?
    The lion dying thrusteth forth his paw
    And wounds the earth, if nothing else, with rage
    To be o'erpowered; and wilt thou, pupil-like,   31
    Take the correction, mildly kiss the rod,
    And fawn on rage with base humility,
    Which art a lion and the king of beasts?   34

KING RICHARD

    A king of beasts, indeed! If aught but beasts,   35
    I had been still a happy king of men.
    Good sometimes queen, prepare thee hence for France.   37
    Think I am dead and that even here thou takest,
    As from my deathbed, thy last living leave.
    In winter's tedious nights sit by the fire
    With good old folks, and let them tell thee tales
    Of woeful ages long ago betid;   42
    And ere thou bid good night, to quit their griefs   43
    Tell thou the lamentable tale of me
    And send the hearers weeping to their beds;
    Forwhy the senseless brands will sympathize   46
    The heavy accent of thy moving tongue,   47
    And in compassion weep the fire out;
    And some will mourn in ashes, some coal-black,   49
    For the deposing of a rightful king.

        Enter Northumberland [attended].

NORTHUMBERLAND

    My lord, the mind of Bolingbroke is changed;
    You must to Pomfret, not unto the Tower.   52
    And, madam, there is order ta'en for you: 53
    With all swift speed you must away to France.

58 **gathering head** gathering to a head

59 **corruption** putrid matter, pus.

61 **helping** since you helped

64 **Being . . . way** though scarcely urged at all

65 **To** how to

66 **converts** changes

67 **That fear** i.e., that fear changes.   **one or both** i.e., the new king or his partner, or both

68 **worthy** well-merited

69 **and . . . end** and let the topic be closed on that note.

70 **part . . . part** separate . . . depart

74 **unkiss** annul with a kiss (regarded as the seal of ceremonial bond)

77 **pines the clime** afflicts the climate

80 **Hallowmas** All Saints' Day (November 1), regarded as the beginning of winter.   **short'st of day** the winter solstice.

KING RICHARD

    Northumberland, thou ladder wherewithal
    The mounting Bolingbroke ascends my throne,
    The time shall not be many hours of age
    More than it is ere foul sin, gathering head,   58
    Shall break into corruption. Thou shalt think,   59
    Though he divide the realm and give thee half,
    It is too little, helping him to all;   61
    He shall think that thou, which knowest the way
    To plant unrightful kings, wilt know again,
    Being ne'er so little urged another way,   64
    To pluck him headlong from the usurpèd throne.   65
    The love of wicked men converts to fear,   66
    That fear to hate, and hate turns one or both   67
    To worthy danger and deservèd death.   68

NORTHUMBERLAND

    My guilt be on my head, and there an end.   69
    Take leave and part, for you must part forthwith.   70

KING RICHARD

    Doubly divorced! Bad men, you violate
    A twofold marriage, twixt my crown and me,
    And then betwixt me and my married wife.
    [*To Queen*] Let me unkiss the oath twixt thee and me;   74
    And yet not so, for with a kiss 'twas made.—
    Part us, Northumberland: I towards the north,
    Where shivering cold and sickness pines the clime;   77
    My wife to France, from whence, set forth in pomp,
    She came adornèd hither like sweet May,
    Sent back like Hallowmas or short'st of day.   80

QUEEN

    And must we be divided? Must we part?

KING RICHARD

    Ay, hand from hand, my love, and heart from heart.

QUEEN [*to Northumberland*]

    Banish us both and send the King with me.

84 **policy** political practicality.

88 **Better . . . the near** i.e., better to be far apart than near and yet unable to meet. (The second *near* means "nearer.")

90 **So . . . moans** i.e., Then I will have to sigh and groan all the more, since my journey is longer.

92 **piece . . . out** make the journey seem longer

94 **Since . . . grief** i.e., since wedding ourselves to grief, we embark on a sadness that is only beginning. (A wry joke on the commonplace that a brief and romantic courtship is often the prelude to an interminable marriage.)

95 **and dumbly part** and then let us part in silence

97–8 **'Twere . . . me** It would not be wise of me to take it upon myself

101 **We . . . wanton** We sport with our grief.   **fond** (1) loving (2) pointless, foolish

5.2 *Location: The Duke of York's house.*

NORTHUMBERLAND
That were some love, but little policy.   84

QUEEN
Then whither he goes, thither let me go.

KING RICHARD
So two, together weeping, make one woe.
Weep thou for me in France, I for thee here;
Better far off than, near, be ne'er the near.   88
Go count thy way with sighs, I mine with groans.

QUEEN
So longest way shall have the longest moans.   90

KING RICHARD
Twice for one step I'll groan, the way being short,
And piece the way out with a heavy heart.   92
Come, come, in wooing sorrow let's be brief,
Since, wedding it, there is such length in grief.   94
One kiss shall stop our mouths, and dumbly part;   95
Thus give I mine, and thus take I thy heart.

                                          [*They kiss.*]

QUEEN
Give me mine own again. 'Twere no good part   97
To take on me to keep and kill thy heart.   [*They kiss.*]   98
So, now I have mine own again, begone,
That I may strive to kill it with a groan.

KING RICHARD
We make woe wanton with this fond delay.   101
Once more, adieu! The rest let sorrow say.

                          Exeunt [in two separate groups].

[5.2] ◦◦◦ *Enter Duke of York and the Duchess.*

DUCHESS
My lord, you told me you would tell the rest,

3 **cousins** kinsmen, i.e., nephews (Richard and Bolingbroke)

4 **leave** leave off.

5 **misgoverned** unruly.   **windows' tops** upper windows

9 **Which . . . know** which seemed to know its ambitious rider

16 **With painted imagery** i.e., showing crowds of people, as on a tapestry or painted cloth, depicting a procession. **at once** all together

19 **lower** bowing lower

20 **Bespake** addressed

21 **still** continually

25 **idly** indifferently

When weeping made you break the story off,
Of our two cousins coming into London.   3

YORK
Where did I leave?

DUCHESS   At that sad stop, my lord,   4
Where rude misgoverned hands from windows' tops   5
Threw dust and rubbish on King Richard's head.

YORK
Then, as I said, the Duke, great Bolingbroke,
Mounted upon a hot and fiery steed
Which his aspiring rider seemed to know,   9
With slow but stately pace kept on his course,
Whilst all tongues cried, "God save thee, Bolingbroke!"
You would have thought the very windows spake,
So many greedy looks of young and old
Through casements darted their desiring eyes
Upon his visage, and that all the walls
With painted imagery had said at once,   16
"Jesu preserve thee! Welcome, Bolingbroke!"
Whilst he, from the one side to the other turning,
Bareheaded, lower than his proud steed's neck,   19
Bespake them thus: "I thank you, countrymen."   20
And thus still doing, thus he passed along.   21

DUCHESS
Alack, poor Richard! Where rode he the whilst?

YORK
As in a theater the eyes of men,
After a well-graced actor leaves the stage,
Are idly bent on him that enters next,   25
Thinking his prattle to be tedious,
Even so, or with much more contempt, men's eyes
Did scowl on gentle Richard. No man cried, "God
    save him!"
No joyful tongue gave him his welcome home,
But dust was thrown upon his sacred head—

33 **badges** insignia, outward signs

35 **perforce** necessarily

38 **we . . . contents** i.e., we bind ourselves to be calmly content.

40 **state** i.e., royal title.   **allow** acknowledge.

41 **Aumerle that was** (Aumerle, as a member of Richard's party, lost his dukedom, though he remained Earl of Rutland.)

44 **pledge** the guarantor.   **truth** loyalty

46–7 **Who . . . spring** i.e., Who are the favorites of the new king?

49 **I had . . . one** I'd be just as glad to be left out as to be a favorite at court.

50 **bear you** bear yourself

51 **cropped** plucked, i.e., beheaded

52 **Do . . . hold?** Are those tourneys and pageants going forward? (According to Holinshed, these tourneys at Oxford were part of a conspiracy against Bolingbroke by the Abbot of Westminster and others; the new king was to be invited to attend and there be assassinated.)

Which with such gentle sorrow he shook off,
His face still combating with tears and smiles,
The badges of his grief and patience,   33
That had not God for some strong purpose steeled
The hearts of men, they must _perforce_ have melted,   35
And barbarism itself have pitied him.
But heaven hath a hand in these events,
To whose high will we bound our calm contents.   38
To Bolingbroke are we sworn subjects now,
Whose state and honor I for aye _allow_   40

[Enter Aumerle.]

DUCHESS
Here comes my son Aumerle.

YORK   Aumerle that was;   41
But that is lost for being Richard's friend,
And, madam, you must call him Rutland now.
I am in Parliament pledge for his _truth_   44
And lasting fealty to the new-made king.

DUCHESS
Welcome, my son. Who are the violets now   46
That strew the green lap of the new-come spring?   47

AUMERLE
Madam, I know not, nor I greatly care not.
God knows I had as lief be none as one.   49

YORK
Well, bear you well in this new spring of time,   50
Lest you be cropped before you come to prime.   51
What news from Oxford? Do these jousts and triumphs
  hold?   52

AUMERLE   For aught I know, my lord, they do.

YORK   You will be there, I know.

AUMERLE
If God prevent not, I purpose so.

56 **seal** i.e., seal attached to the border of a document

60 **pardon me** i.e., excuse me if I don't comply.

62 **have seen** wish to be seen.

66 **'gainst** in anticipation of

67–8 **What . . . bound to?** i.e., Why would *he* have the
   bond instead of the creditor to whom the debt is owed?

75 **God** i.e., I pray God

YORK
What seal is that, that hangs without thy bosom?   56
Yea, look'st thou pale? Let me see the writing.

AUMERLE
My lord, 'tis nothing.

YORK   No matter, then, who see it.
I will be satisfied. Let me see the writing.

AUMERLE
I do beseech Your Grace to pardon me.   60
It is a matter of small consequence,
Which for some reasons I would not have seen.   62

YORK
Which for some reasons, sir, I mean to see.
I fear, I fear—

DUCHESS   What should you fear?
'Tis nothing but some bond that he is entered into
For gay apparel 'gainst the triumph day.   66

In anticipation of

YORK
Bound to himself? What doth he with a bond   67
That he is bound to? Wife, thou art a fool.—   68
Boy, let me see the writing.

AUMERLE
I do beseech you, pardon me. I may not show it.

YORK
I will be satisfied. Let me see it, I say.

                    He plucks it out of his bosom and reads it.

Treason! Foul treason! Villain! Traitor! Slave!

DUCHESS   What is the matter, my lord?

YORK [*calling offstage*] Ho! Who is within there?

          [*Enter a Servingman.*]

                    Saddle my horse!—
God for his mercy, what treachery is here?   75

DUCHESS   Why, what is it, my lord?

78 **troth** faith, allegiance

79 **appeach** inform against, publicly accuse

85 **Strike him** i.e., Strike the servant.   **amazed** confused, bewildered.

90 **Have we more sons?** (Historically, this Duchess of York was the Duke's second wife and was not Aumerle's mother; she was, however, the mother of another son, Richard, subsequently Earl of Cambridge.)

91 **teeming date** period of childbearing

95 **fond** foolish

YORK [*to the Servingman*]
     Give me my boots, I say! Saddle my horse!—

                              [*Exit Servingman.*]

     Now, by mine honor, by my life, my troth,   78
     I will appeach the villain.

DUCHESS   What is the matter?   79

YORK
     Peace, foolish woman.

DUCHESS
     I will not peace. What is the matter, Aumerle?

AUMERLE
     Good mother, be content. It is no more
     Than my poor life must answer.

DUCHESS   Thy life answer?

YORK [*calling*]
     Bring me my boots! I will unto the King.

          His [Serving]man enters with his boots.

DUCHESS
     Strike him, Aumerle. Poor boy, thou art amazed.   85
     [*To the Servingman*] Hence, villain! Never more come
          in my sight.

YORK   Give me my boots, I say.

     [*The Servingman helps him on with his boots, and exit.*]

DUCHESS   Why, York, what wilt thou do?
     Wilt thou not hide the trespass of thine own?
     Have we more sons? Or are we like to have?   90
     Is not my teeming date drunk up with time?   91
     And wilt thou pluck my fair son from mine age
     And rob me of a happy mother's name?
     Is he not like thee? Is he not thine own?

YORK   Thou fond mad woman,   95
     Wilt thou conceal this dark conspiracy?

97–9 **A dozen . . . Oxford** ("Hereupon was an indenture
sextipartite made, sealed with their seals and signed
with their hands, in the which each stood bound to
other, to do their whole endeavor for the accomplish-
ing of their purposed exploit." [Holinshed])

100 **that** i.e., the plot

102 **groaned for** i.e., given birth to. (But see note, line 90.)

103 **pitiful** pitying.

111 **After** Go after him.   **his horse** i.e., one of York's
horses

112 **Spur post** ride as fast as possible

5.3 *Location: The court (i.e., Windsor Castle).*
  1 **unthrifty** profligate

A dozen of them here have ta'en the Sacrament,   97
And interchangeably set down their hands,   98
To kill the King at Oxford.

DUCHESS   He shall be none;   99
We'll keep him here. Then what is that to him?   100

YORK
Away, fond woman! Were he twenty times my son
I would appeach him.

DUCHESS   Hadst thou groaned for him   102
As I have done, thou wouldst be more pitiful.   103
But now I know thy mind. Thou dost suspect
That I have been disloyal to thy bed,
And that he is a bastard, not thy son.
Sweet York, sweet husband, be not of that mind!
He is as like thee as a man may be,
Not like to me, or any of my kin,
And yet I love him.

YORK   Make way, unruly woman! *Exit.*

DUCHESS
After, Aumerle! Mount thee upon his horse,   111
Spur post, and get before him to the King,   112
And beg thy pardon ere he do accuse thee.
I'll not be long behind. Though I be old,
I doubt not but to ride as fast as York.
And never will I rise up from the ground
Till Bolingbroke have pardoned thee. Away, begone!

                    [*Exeunt separately.*]

[5.3] ⤳ *Enter* [*Bolingbroke, now*] *King* [*Henry*], *with his
                    nobles* [*Harry Percy and others*].

KING HENRY   profligate
Can no man tell me of my <u>unthrifty</u> son?   1
'Tis full three months since I did see him last.

9 **watch** night watchmen.   **passengers** passers-by, way-farers

10 **wanton** pampered youth.   **effeminate** self-indulgent

11 **Takes on the** i.e., makes it a

14 **held** i.e., to be held

16 **stews** brothels

17 **common'st** most promiscuous

18 **with that** i.e., wearing that as a favor

19 **lustiest** most vigorous and brave

22 **happily** with good fortune

22.1 *amazed* distraught.

If any plague hang over us, 'tis he.
I would to God, my lords, he might be found.
Inquire at London, 'mongst the taverns there,
For there, they say, he daily doth frequent
With unrestrainèd loose companions,
Even such, they say, as stand in narrow lanes
And beat our watch, and rob our passengers— 9
While he, young wanton and effeminate boy, 10
Takes on the point of honor to support 11
So dissolute a crew.

PERCY
My lord, some two days since I saw the Prince,
And told him of those triumphs held at Oxford. 14

KING HENRY And what said the gallant?

PERCY
His answer was, he would unto the stews, 16
And from the common'st creature pluck a glove, 17
And wear it as a favor, and with that 18
He would unhorse the lustiest challenger. 19

KING HENRY
As dissolute as desperate! Yet through both
I see some sparks of better hope, which elder years
May happily bring forth. But who comes here? 22

Enter Aumerle, amazed.

AUMERLE Where is the King?

KING HENRY
What means our cousin, that he stares and looks
So wildly?

AUMERLE
God save Your Grace! I do beseech Your Majesty
To have some conference with Your Grace alone.

KING HENRY [*to his nobles*]
Withdraw yourselves, and leave us here alone.

31 **My . . . mouth** (See Psalm 137:6: "If I do not remember thee, let my tongue cleave to the roof of my mouth.")

34 **If on the first** i.e., If intended only

41 **I'll . . . safe** I'll make you harmless (by running you through).

43 **secure** unsuspecting, heedless

44 **speak . . . face** i.e., speak so disrespectfully as to call you *secure* and *foolhardy*.

                              [*Exeunt Percy and lords.*]

What is the matter with our cousin now?

AUMERLE [*kneeling*]
Forever may my knees grow to the earth,
My tongue cleave to the roof within my mouth,   31
Unless a pardon ere I rise or speak.

KING HENRY
Intended or committed was this fault?
If on the first, how heinous e'er it be,   34
To win thy after-love I pardon thee.

AUMERLE [*rising*]
Then give me leave that I may turn the key,
That no man enter till my tale be done.

KING HENRY   Have thy desire.
                    [*Aumerle locks the door.*]   *The Duke of York*
                                knocks at the door and crieth.

YORK [*within*]
My liege, beware! Look to thyself.
Thou hast a traitor in thy presence there.

KING HENRY [*drawing*]   Villain, I'll make thee safe.   41

AUMERLE
Stay thy revengeful hand. Thou hast no cause to fear.

YORK [*within*]
Open the door, secure, foolhardy King!   43
Shall I for love speak treason to thy face?   44
Open the door, or I will break it open.

                              [*King Henry unlocks the door.*]

        [*Enter York.*]

KING HENRY
What is the matter, uncle? Speak.
Recover breath; tell us how near is danger,
That we may arm us to encounter it.

50 **haste. . . show** i.e., breathlessness prevents me from revealing.

53 **hand** signature.

57 **Forget** Forget your promise

61 **sheer** clear, pure

63 **himself** (1) itself (2) himself, Aumerle

64 **Thy . . . bad** your excess of goodness atones for what is bad (in Aumerle)

66 **digressing** deviating from his proper course, transgressing

69 **scraping** parsimonious

71 **in . . . lies** will be hostage to his dishonorable conduct.

72 **in his life** if you permit him to live

YORK [*giving letter*]
    Peruse this writing here, and thou shalt know
    The treason that my haste forbids me show.   50

AUMERLE
    Remember, as thou read'st, thy promise passed.
    I do repent me. Read not my name there;
    My heart is not confederate with my hand.   53

YORK
    It was, villain, ere thy hand did set it down.
    I tore it from the traitor's bosom, King;
    Fear, and not love, begets his penitence.
    Forget to pity him, lest thy pity prove   57
    A serpent that will sting thee to the heart.

KING HENRY
    Oh, heinous, strong, and bold conspiracy!
    O loyal father of a treacherous son,
    Thou sheer, immaculate, and silver fountain,   61
    From whence this stream through muddy passages
    Hath held his current and defiled himself,   63
    Thy overflow of good converts to bad,   64
    And thy abundant goodness shall excuse
    This deadly blot in thy digressing son.   66

YORK
    So shall my virtue be his vice's bawd,
    And he shall spend mine honor with his shame,
    As thriftless sons their scraping fathers' gold.   69
    Mine honor lives when his dishonor dies,
    Or my shamed life in his dishonor lies.   71
    Thou kill'st me in his life; giving him breath,   72
    The traitor lives, the true man's put to death.

DUCHESS [*within*]
    What ho, my liege! For God's sake, let me in.

KING HENRY
    What shrill-voiced suppliant makes this eager cry?

80 **"The Beggar . . . King"** (Probably one of Shakespeare's
many allusions to the ballad of King Cophetua and the
Beggar Maid.)

83 **whosoever pray** anyone who presents a petition

84 **for** because of

86 **alone** untreated.   **confound** ruin.

88 **Love . . . can** i.e., He who does not love himself in his
own son can love no one else, not even the King.

89 **make** do

90 **once . . . rear** i.e., give life again to a traitor by now re-
deeming Aumerle from death.

94 **And . . . sees** and never enjoy the happiness that those
who are happy experience

97 **Unto** In support of

DUCHESS [*within*]
    A woman, and thy aunt, great King. 'Tis I.
    Speak with me, pity me, open the door!
    A beggar begs that never begged before.

KING HENRY
    Our scene is altered from a serious thing,
    And now changed to "The Beggar and the King."   80
    My dangerous cousin, let your mother in.
    I know she is come to pray for your foul sin.

        [*Aumerle opens the door. Enter the Duchess. She
        kneels.*]

YORK
    If thou do pardon whosoever pray,   83
    More sins for this forgiveness prosper may.   84
    This festered joint cut off, the rest rest sound;
    This let alone will all the rest confound. ruin   86

DUCHESS
    O King, believe not this hardhearted man.
    Love loving not itself, none other can.   88

YORK
    Thou frantic woman, what dost thou make here?   89
    Shall thy old dugs once more a traitor rear?   90

DUCHESS
    Sweet York, be patient.—Hear me, gentle liege.

KING HENRY
    Rise up, good aunt.

DUCHESS   Not yet, I thee beseech.
    Forever will I walk upon my knees,
    And never see day that the happy sees,   94
    Till thou give joy, until thou bid me joy,
    By pardoning Rutland, my transgressing boy.

AUMERLE [*kneeling*]
    Unto my mother's prayers I bend my knee.   97

104 **beside** besides.

106 **still** continually

113 **An if** If

119 **pardonne moy** *pardonnez-moi,* excuse me. (An affect-
edly polite refusal.)

124 **chopping** logic chopping, changing the sense

YORK [*kneeling*]

    Against them both my true joints bended be.

    Ill mayst thou thrive, if thou grant any grace!

DUCHESS

    Pleads he in earnest? Look upon his face.

    His eyes do drop no tears, his prayers are in jest;

    His words come from his mouth, ours from our breast.

    He prays but faintly and would be denied;

    We pray with heart and soul and all beside.   104

    His weary joints would gladly rise, I know;

    Our knees still kneel till to the ground they grow.   106

    His prayers are full of false hypocrisy,

    Ours of true zeal and deep integrity.

    Our prayers do outpray his; then let them have

    That mercy which true prayer ought to have.

KING HENRY

    Good aunt, stand up.

DUCHESS   Nay, do not say "stand up."

    Say "pardon" first, and afterwards "stand up."

    An if I were thy nurse, thy tongue to teach,   113

    "Pardon" should be the first word of thy speech.

    I never longed to hear a word till now;

    Say "pardon," King; let pity teach thee how.

    The word is short, but not so short as sweet;

    No word like "pardon" for kings' mouths so meet.

YORK

    Speak it in French, King: say "pardonne moy."   119

DUCHESS

    Dost thou teach pardon pardon to destroy?

    Ah, my sour husband, my hardhearted lord,

    That sets the word itself against the word!

    Speak "pardon" as 'tis current in our land;

    The chopping French we do not understand.   124

    Thine eye begins to speak; set thy tongue there,

    Or in thy piteous heart plant thou thine ear,

128 **rehearse** pronounce.

132 **happy vantage** fortunate gain

137 **But for** But as for.   **brother-in-law** i.e., John Holland, Earl of Huntington and Duke of Exeter, who had married Bolingbroke's sister (see 2.1.281 and note).   **Abbot** Abbot of Westminster; see 4.1.321-34

138 **consorted** conspiring, confederate

140 **powers** forces

145 **prove you true** may you prove loyal.

146 **old** unregenerate

5.4 *Location: The court.* (The opening stage direction in the quarto reads *Manet Sir Pierce Exton, etc.*, suggesting continuity of action with the preceding scene.)

That hearing how our plaints and prayers do pierce,
Pity may move thee "pardon" to rehearse.   128

KING HENRY
Good aunt, stand up.

DUCHESS   I do not sue to stand.
Pardon is all the suit I have in hand.

KING HENRY
I pardon him, as God shall pardon me.

DUCHESS
Oh, happy vantage of a kneeling knee!   132
Yet am I sick for fear. Speak it again;
Twice saying "pardon" doth not pardon twain
But makes one pardon strong.

KING HENRY   With all my heart
I pardon him.   [All rise.]

DUCHESS   A god on earth thou art.

KING HENRY
But for our trusty brother-in-law and the Abbot,   137
With all the rest of that consorted crew,   138
Destruction straight shall dog them at the heels.
Good uncle, help to order several powers   140
To Oxford, or where'er these traitors are.
They shall not live within this world, I swear,
But I will have them, if I once know where.
Uncle, farewell, and, cousin, adieu.
Your mother well hath prayed; and prove you true.   145

DUCHESS
Come, my old son. I pray God make thee new.   146
                    Exeunt [in two groups].

[5.4] ❧ *Enter Sir Pierce [of] Exton [and his Men].*

EXTON
Didst thou not mark the King, what words he spake,

   2 **will** who will
   7 **wishtly** intently
   8 **As . . . say** as if to say
 11 **rid** rid him of

5.5 *Location: Pomfret Castle. A dungeon.*
   3 **for because** because
   5 **hammer** i.e., work, puzzle
   8 **still-breeding** constantly breeding
   9 **this little world** myself and this prison as a microcosm
     of the world
 10 **humors** temperaments, peculiar fancies
 12 **As** such as
 13 **scruples** doubts
13–14 **do set . . . word** i.e., oppose one scriptural passage
    against its apparent opposite
14–17 **Come . . . eye** (See Matthew 19:14, 24.)

"Have I no friend will rid me of this living fear?"   2
Was it not so?

MAN   These were his very words.

EXTON

"Have I no friend?" quoth he. He spake it twice,
And urged it twice together, did he not?

MAN   He did.

EXTON

And speaking it, he wishtly looked on me,   7
As who should say, "I would thou wert the man   8
That would divorce this terror from my heart"—
Meaning the King at Pomfret. Come, let's go.
I am the King's friend, and will rid his foe.   11

[Exeunt.]

[5.5] ✜ *Enter Richard alone.*

KING RICHARD

I have been studying how I may compare
This prison where I live unto the world;
And, for because the world is populous,   3
And here is not a creature but myself,
I cannot do it. Yet I'll hammer it out.   5
My brain I'll prove the female to my soul,
My soul the father, and these two beget
A generation of still-breeding thoughts;   8
And these same thoughts people this little world,   9
In humors like the people of this world,   10
For no thought is contented. The better sort,
As thoughts of things divine, are intermixed   12
With scruples and do set the word itself   13
Against the word, as thus, "Come, little ones,"   14
And then again,
"It is as hard to come as for a camel

17 **postern** narrow gate

21 **ragged** rugged

22 **for** because.   **pride** prime.

23 **content** contentment

25 **seely** simpleminded

26 **refuge their shame** i.e., seek refuge from their disgrace by reflecting

33 **treason** i.e., the thought of treason

34 **penury** poverty

39–41 **Nor . . . nothing** neither I nor any person alive can be fully satisfied with the things of this life until he or she is released by death.

46 **check** rebuke.   **string** stringed instrument

50 **numb'ring clock** i.e., a clock that numbers hours and minutes (not an hourglass).

To thread the postern of a small needle's eye."   17
Thoughts tending to ambition, they do plot
Unlikely wonders—how these vain weak nails
May tear a passage through the flinty ribs
Of this hard world, my ragged prison walls,   21
And, for they cannot, die in their own pride.   22
Thoughts tending to content flatter themselves   23
That they are not the first of fortune's slaves,
Nor shall not be the last—like seely beggars   25
Who, sitting in the stocks, refuge their shame   26
That many have and others must sit there;
And in this thought they find a kind of ease,
Bearing their own misfortunes on the back
Of such as have before endured the like.
Thus play I in one person many people,
And none contented. Sometimes am I king;
Then treason makes me wish myself a beggar,   33
And so I am. Then crushing penury   34
Persuades me I was better when a king;
Then am I kinged again, and by and by
Think that I am unkinged by Bolingbroke,
And straight am nothing. But whate'er I be,
Nor I, nor any man that but man is,   39
With nothing shall be pleased till he be eased   40
With being nothing. (*The music plays*.) Music do I
    hear?   41
Ha, ha, keep time! How sour sweet music is
When time is broke and no proportion kept!
So is it in the music of men's lives.
And here have I the daintiness of ear
To check time broke in a disordered string,   46
But for the concord of my state and time
Had not an ear to hear my true time broke.
I wasted time, and now doth time waste me;
For now hath Time made me his numb'ring clock.   50

51–2 **My . . . watch** My sad thoughts, occurring every minute, are parts of an inner clock that, by means of the sighs they provoke, transfer their cares to my eyes, the face of the clock

53 **dial's point** clock hand

58 **times** quarters and halves.

59 **posting** hastening

60 **jack of the clock** manikin that struck the bell on a clock.

61 **mads** maddens

62 **holp** helped

66 **strange brooch** rare jewel

68 **ten groats too dear** (There is a pun on *royal* and *noble* in the preceding lines. A royal (ten shillings) is worth ten groats (ten times four pence) more than a noble (six shillings, eight pence) is; hence, Richard is saying that he, "the cheapest of us" because he is a prisoner, is worth no more than the groom, whom he greets as his "noble peer.")

75 **sometimes** former

76 **earned** grieved

My thoughts are minutes, and with sighs they jar   51
Their watches on unto mine eyes, the outward watch   52
Whereto my finger, like a dial's point,   53
Is pointing still in cleansing them from tears.
Now sir, the sounds that tell what hour it is
Are clamorous groans that strike upon my heart,
Which is the bell. So sighs and tears and groans
Show minutes, hours, and times. But my time   58
Runs posting on in Bolingbroke's proud joy,   59
While I stand fooling here, his jack of the clock.   60
This music mads me. Let it sound no more,   61
For though it have holp madmen to their wits,   62
In me it seems it will make wise men mad.

                                    [*The music ceases.*]

Yet blessing on his heart that gives it me!
For 'tis a sign of love; and love to Richard
Is a strange brooch in this all-hating world.   66

        Enter a Groom of the stable.

GROOM
  Hail, royal prince!
KING RICHARD   Thanks, noble peer.
  The cheapest of us is ten groats too dear.   68
  What art thou, and how comest thou hither,
  Where no man never comes but that sad dog
  That brings me food to make misfortune live?

GROOM
  I was a poor groom of thy stable, King,
  When thou wert king; who, traveling towards York,
  With much ado at length have gotten leave
  To look upon my sometimes royal master's face.   75
  Oh, how it earned my heart when I beheld   76
  In London streets, that coronation day,
  When Bolingbroke rode on roan Barbary,

80 **dressed** tended, groomed.

85 **eat** eaten. (Pronounced "et.")

86 **clapping** patting, stroking

94 **galled** made sore.   **jauncing** prancing, hard-riding

94.1 *meat* food.

99 **Taste . . . first** i.e., to ensure that it isn't poisoned

That horse that thou so often hast bestrid,
That horse that I so carefully have dressed!   80

KING RICHARD
Rode he on Barbary? Tell me, gentle friend,
How went he under him?

GROOM
So proudly as if he disdained the ground.

KING RICHARD
So proud that Bolingbroke was on his back!
That jade hath eat bread from my royal hand;   85
This hand hath made him proud with clapping him.   86
Would he not stumble? Would he not fall down,
Since pride must have a fall, and break the neck
Of that proud man that did usurp his back?
Forgiveness, horse! Why do I rail on thee,
Since thou, created to be awed by man,
Wast born to bear? I was not made a horse,
And yet I bear a burden like an ass,
Spurred, galled, and tired by jauncing Bolingbroke.   94

Enter one [a Keeper] to Richard with meat.

KEEPER [*to Groom*]
Fellow, give place. Here is no longer stay.

KING RICHARD [*to Groom*]
If thou love me, 'tis time thou wert away.

GROOM
What my tongue dares not, that my heart shall say.
                                        Exit Groom.

KEEPER
My lord, will't please you to fall to?

KING RICHARD
Taste of it first, as thou art wont to do.   99

107 **room** place
109 **staggers** causes to stagger

KEEPER

    My lord, I dare not. Sir Pierce of Exton, who
    Lately came from the King, commands the contrary.

KING RICHARD

    The devil take Henry of Lancaster and thee!
    Patience is stale, and I am weary of it.

                        [He beats the Keeper.]

KEEPER   Help, help, help!

       The murderers [Exton and his men] rush in.

KING RICHARD

    How now, what means death in this rude assault?
    Villain, thy own hand yields thy death's instrument.

        [He snatches a weapon from a man and kills him.]

    Go thou, and fill another room in hell.   107

        [He kills another.] Here Exton strikes him down.

    That hand shall burn in never-quenching fire
    That staggers thus my person. Exton, thy fierce hand   109
    Hath with the King's blood stained the King's own
       land.
    Mount, mount, my soul! Thy seat is up on high,
    Whilst my gross flesh sinks downward, here to die.

                            [He dies.]

EXTON

    As full of valor as of royal blood.
    Both have I spilled. Oh, would the deed were good!
    For now the devil, that told me I did well,
    Says that this deed is chronicled in hell.
    This dead king to the living king I'll bear.
    Take hence the rest, and give them burial here.

                    [Exeunt, with the bodies.]

5.6 *Location: The court.*

  3 **Ci'cester** Cirencester

  9 **taking** capture

10 **At large discoursèd** related in full

12 **worth** (1) deserving (2) present wealth

15 **consorted** conspiring

18 **wot** know.

[5.6] ❧ [*Flourish.*] *Enter Bolingbroke [as King], with the*
Duke of York, [other lords, and attendants].

KING HENRY
  Kind uncle York, the latest news we hear
  Is that the rebels have consumed with fire
  Our town of Ci'cester in Gloucestershire,   3
  But whether they be ta'en or slain we hear not.

      Enter Northumberland.

  Welcome, my lord. What is the news?

NORTHUMBERLAND
  First, to thy sacred state wish I all happiness.
  The next news is, I have to London sent
  The heads of Salisbury, Spencer, Blunt, and Kent.
  The manner of their taking may appear   9
  At large discoursèd in this paper here.   10

                      [*He gives a paper.*]

KING HENRY
  We thank thee, gentle Percy, for thy pains,
  And to thy worth will add right worthy gains.   12

      Enter Lord Fitzwater.

FITZWATER
  My lord, I have from Oxford sent to London
  The heads of Brocas and Sir Bennet Seely,
  Two of the dangerous consorted traitors   15
  That sought at Oxford thy dire overthrow.

KING HENRY
  Thy pains, Fitzwater, shall not be forgot;
  Right noble is thy merit, well I wot.   18

19 **grand** chief

20 **clog** burden

22 **abide** await

23 **doom** judgment

25 **reverent room** place suitable for religious retirement

26 **More than thou hast** i.e., larger than your present cell, or more worthy of reverence.   **joy** enjoy, have the benefit of

27 **So as** Provided that

35 **deed of slander** i.e., a deed sure to arouse slanderous talk about the new King

43 **Cain** murderer of his brother Abel; see 1.1.104

Enter Henry Percy [with the Bishop of Carlisle, guarded].

PERCY
The grand conspirator, Abbot of Westminster,   19
With clog of conscience and sour melancholy   20
Hath yielded up his body to the grave;
But here is Carlisle living, to abide   22
Thy kingly doom and sentence of his pride.   23

KING HENRY   Carlisle, this is your doom:
Choose out some secret place, some reverent room,   25
More than thou hast, and with it joy thy life.   26
So as thou liv'st in peace, die free from strife;   27
For though mine enemy thou hast ever been,
High sparks of honor in thee have I seen.

Enter Exton, with [attendants bearing] the coffin.

EXTON
Great King, within this coffin I present
Thy buried fear. Herein all breathless lies
The mightiest of thy greatest enemies,
Richard of Bordeaux, by me hither brought.

KING HENRY
Exton, I thank thee not, for thou hast wrought
A deed of slander with thy fatal hand   35
Upon my head and all this famous land.

EXTON
From your own mouth, my lord, did I this deed.

KING HENRY
They love not poison that do poison need,
Nor do I thee. Though I did wish him dead,
I hate the murderer, love him murderèd.
The guilt of conscience take thou for thy labor,
But neither my good word nor princely favor.
With Cain go wander through the shades of night,   43

48 **incontinent** immediately.
51 **Grace** Dignify

And never show thy head by day nor light.

                  [Exeunt Exton and attendants.]

Lords, I protest my soul is full of woe
That blood should sprinkle me to make me grow.
Come mourn with me for what I do lament,
And put on sullen black incontinent.   48
I'll make a voyage to the Holy Land
To wash this blood off from my guilty hand.
March sadly after. Grace my mournings here   51
In weeping after this untimely bier.

             [Exeunt in procession, following the coffin.]

DATE AND TEXT

On August 29, 1597, "The Tragedye of Richard the Second" was entered in the Stationers' Register, the official record book of the London Company of Stationers (booksellers and printers), by Andrew Wise, and was published by him later that same year:

THE Tragedie of King Richard the second. *As it hath beene publikely acted by the right Honourable the Lorde Chamberlaine his Seruants.* LONDON Printed by Valentine Simmes for Androw Wise, and are to be sold at his shop in Paules church yard at the signe of the Angel. 1597.

This is a good text, printed evidently from the author's papers or a nontheatrical transcript of them. Wise issued two more quartos of this popular play in 1598, each set from the previous quarto, and then in 1603 transferred his rights to the play to Matthew Law. This publisher issued in 1608 a fourth quarto "With new additions of the Parliament Sceane, and the deposing of King Richard" (according to the title page in some copies). The deposition scene has indeed been omitted from the earlier quartos, probably through censorship. A fifth quarto appeared in 1615, based on the fourth quarto. All the quartos after the first attribute the play to Shakespeare. The added deposition scene in quartos 4 and 5 seems to have been memorially reconstructed. The First Folio text of 1623 gives a better version of the deposition scene, seemingly because the printers of the Folio had access to the manuscript playbook for this portion of the text. (Some scholars maintain that the Folio text was derived from an earlier quarto or quartos that had been marked up and used as a playbook, but that case has been weakened by recent research.) Most of the Folio text was probably set from an annotated copy of the third quarto, and perhaps a leaf in act 5 from the fifth quarto. The annotation was evidently quite uneven, and so the most authoritative text for all but the deposition scene remains the first quarto; nevertheless, at certain points (especially the first 900 lines, part of 3.2, and much of act 5), the annotation with reference to the playbook seems to have been more thorough. At such points, the Folio readings deserve serious attention, and the stage directions are often illuminating.

Francis Meres mentions the play in 1598 in his *Palladis Tamia*. Clearly it had been written and performed prior to the Stationers' Register entry in August 1597. Its earliest probable date is 1595, since the play seemingly is indebted to Samuel Daniel's poem, *The First Four Books of the Civil Wars*, published in that year. Shakespeare follows Daniel, for example, in increasing the Queen's age from eleven (according to the chronicles) to maturity, and in other significant details. On December 7, 1595, Sir Edward Hoby invited Sir Robert Cecil to his house in Cannon Row, "where as late as it shall please you a gate for your supper shall be open, and King Richard present himself to your view." Although it is by no means certain that this passage refers to a private performance of Shakespeare's play, stylistic considerations favor a date around 1595 rather than 1597. If, as some scholars contend, Daniel's *Civil Wars* was written after Shakespeare's play rather than before it, the date of *Richard II* might be as early as 1594.

TEXTUAL NOTES

These textual notes are not a historical collation, either of the early quartos and the early folios or of more recent editions; they are simply a record of departures in this edition from the copy text. The reading adopted in this edition appears in boldface, followed by the rejected reading from the copy text, i.e., the quarto of 1597. Only major alterations in punctuation are noted. Changes in lineation are not indicated, nor are some minor and obvious typographical errors.

Copy text: the first quarto of 1597 as press-corrected in all four extant copies [Q1]; and, for the deposition scene, 4.1. 155–321, the First Folio. Act and scene divisions, absent in Q1, are from F except that F provides no scene marking at 5.4 and labels 5.5 and 5.6 as "*Scoena Quarta*" and "*Scoena Quinta*," respectively.

1.1. 15 presence. Face presence face   **19.1 [and throughout]** *Bolingbroke* Bullingbrooke   **118 by my** [F] by   **139 But** Ah but   **152 gentlemen** [F] gentleman   **162–3 Harry, when? / Obedience bids** Harry? when obedience bids. / Obedience bids   **176 gage. My** gage, my   **178 reputation; that** Reputation that   **192 parle** parlee   **205.1** *Exeunt* Exit

1.2. 25 him. Thou him, thou   **42 alas** [not in Q]   **47 sit** [F] set   **48 butcher** [Qb, F] butchers [Qa]   **58 it** [Q2–5, F] is   **59 empty** [Qb, F] emptines, [Qa]   **60 begun** begone   **70 hear** [F] cheere

1.3. 15 thee the   **33 comest** [Q5] comes   **58 thee** the   **104 FIRST HERALD** *Herald*   **108 his God** [F] God   **128 civil** [Qb, F] cruel [Qa]   **133 Draws** [Qb] Draw [Qa]   **136 wrathful iron** [Qb, F] harsh resounding [Qa]   **172 then but** [F] but   **180 you owe** [F] y'owe   **193 far** fare   **222 night** [Q4–5, F] nightes   **239 had it** had't   **241 sought** ought   **269 world** world:

1.4. 0.1 *Bagot* [F] *Bushie*   **20 our cousin,** [F] our Coosens   **23 Bagot here, and Green** [Q6; not in Q1]   **27 What** [Qb, F] With

[Qa]   47 hand. If hand if   52.1 *Enter Bushy* [F] *Enter Bushie with newes*   53 Bushy, what news [F; not in Q1]   65 ALL [not in Q1]

2.1. 15 life's liues   18 fond found   30 [and elsewhere] lose loose
48 as a [Q4–5, F] as   68.1–2 [after line 70 in Q1]   70 reined
ragde   102 encagèd [F] inraged   113 not not, not   124 brother
brothers   156 kerns [Qb, F] kerne   161 coin [Qb, F] coines [Qa]
168 my [Qb, F] mine   177 the [F] a   209 seize cease
239 more mo   257 King's [Q3–5, F] King   277 Port le Blanc le
Port Blan   278 Brittany Brittaine [also in 285]   284 Coint
Coines

2.2. 19 Show [Q6, F] Shows [Qa]   31 though [Q2–5, F] thought
53 Harry H.

2.3. 9 Cotswold Cotshall   30 Lordship Lo: 36 Hereford [Q3–5,
F] Herefords   75 raze race   99 the lord [F] Lord   164 [and
elsewhere] Bristol Bristow

2.4. 1 WELSH CAPTAIN *Welsh* [also at line 7]

3.2. 32 succor succors   40 boldly bouldy   72 O'erthrows [F]
Ouerthrowes   86 name! A name a   170 through [Q2–5, F]
thorough

3.3. 13 brief with you [F] briefe   31 lord [F] Lords   59 rain
raigne.   60 waters—on water's on   100 pastures' pastors
119 a prince and princesse   127 ourself our selues

3.4. 11 joy griefe   26 pins [F] pines   27 state, for state for
28 change; woe change woe   29 apricots Aphricokes   34 too [F]
two   48 hath htah   55 Seized ceasde   57 We at at
80 Cam'st [Q2–5, F] Canst

4.1. 23 him [Q3–5, F] them   44 Fitzwater [F] Fitzwaters   55 As
As it   56 sun to sun sinne to sinne   63 true. You true you
77 my bond [Q3–5, F] bond   110 thee [Q2–5, F] the   146 you
yon   155–321 [This deposition scene is based on the First Folio
text; Q1 has only: "Let it be so, and loe on Wednesday next, / We
solemnly proclaime our Coronation, / Lords be ready all." Unless
otherwise indicated, all the departures in F from lines 155–321 are
taken from Q4.]   184 and on on   252 and a   256 Nor No,
nor   297 manners manner   321.2 *Carlisle Caleil*

5.1. 11 model modle   41 thee [Q2–5, F] the
84 NORTHUMBERLAND [F] *King*

5.2. 2 off [F] of   **11 thee** [F] the [also at lines 17 and 94]   **78 my troth** by my troth   **94 thee** the   **116 And** An

5.3. 0.1 King *the* King   **10 While** Which   **31 the** my   **36 I may** [Q2–5, F] May   **68 And** An   **75 shrill-voiced** shrill voice
111 KING HENRY *yorke*   **135–6 With . . . him** I pardon him with al my heart

5.4. 0.1 Enter [F] *Manet*   **Exton** Exton, *etc.*

5.5. 20 through [F] thorow   **22 cannot, die** cannot die   **27 sit** [Q3–5, F] set   **33 treason makes** treasons make   **55 sounds that tell** sound that telles   **56 that** which   **58 hours, and times** times, and houres

5.6. 8 Salisbury, Spencer [F] Oxford, Salisbury   **12.1 Fitzwater** *Fitzwaters*   **43 through the** [F] through

SHAKESPEARE'S SOURCES

Shakespeare's primary source for *Richard II* was the 1587 edition of Raphael Holinshed's *Chronicles* covering the years 1398 to 1400. As in his earlier *Henry VI* plays and *Richard III*, Shakespeare departs from historical accuracy in the interests of artistic design. Queen Isabel's part is almost wholly invented, for historically she was a child of eleven at the time the events in this play occurred. Her "Garden Scene" (3.4) is a fine piece of invention, bringing together images of order and disorder that are found in the rest of the play. The Duchess of York's role is entirely original; Holinshed reports the scene in which York's son Aumerle (the Earl of Rutland) rides to the new King and begs for mercy while his father simultaneously denounces him as a traitor, but the Duchess is never mentioned. Shakespeare has added the poignant conflict between husband and wife. Northumberland's role as conspirator against Richard and as hatchet man for Bolingbroke is greatly enlarged; for example, Holinshed never names the persons who engage in the original plotting against Richard. Yet Shakespeare's Bolingbroke returns to England on his own initiative, whereas in Holinshed he does so at the barons' invitation, a change that accentuates the puzzle of Bolingbroke's motive. Another invention is the meeting between John of Gaunt and the Duchess of Gloucester (1.2). In fact, most of Gaunt's character and behavior have no basis in Holinshed at all. Shakespeare creates him to fill the role of thoughtfully conservative statesman, agonized by his son's banishment but doggedly obedient to his monarch. Finally, and most important, Shakespeare has greatly enlarged the role and the poetic nature of King Richard, especially in the final two acts.

Many of these alterations are Shakespeare's own; others derive from his reading in other sources. Samuel Daniel's *The First Four Books of the Civil Wars* (1595) may have had an important influence. Although we cannot discount the possibility that

Shakespeare's play may have been written first, the consensus today is that he knew Daniel's poem. It gave him the idea of the Queen's maturity and grief (although not the Garden Scene) and the final meeting of King and Queen. Daniel's Hotspur is unhistorically a young man, as in act 2, scene 3 of Shakespeare's play. Like Shakespeare, Daniel sees York as a man of "a mild temperateness." Daniel's Richard and Bolingbroke ride together into London, not separately as in Holinshed. In Daniel's poem, Bolingbroke's indirect manner of insinuating his desire for Richard's death ("And wished that some would so his life esteem / As rid him of these fears wherein he stood") is verbally close to Shakespeare's depiction of this scene. Richard's final soliloquies in these two works show an unmistakable similarity to one another.

Richard II's reign was a controversial subject in the 1590s and produced other plays of varying political coloration that Shakespeare must have known. *The Life and Death of Jack Straw* (anonymous, 1590–1593) distorts history in its friendly portrayal of Richard's role in the Peasants' Revolt of 1381, and whitewashes governmental policy. In contrast, the anonymous play *Thomas of Woodstock*, sometimes known as *1 Richard II* (1591–1595), is almost a call for open rebellion against tyranny. Many verbal similarities link this latter play with Shakespeare's *Richard II*, and although scholars have difficulty in determining which was written first, the wary consensus is that Shakespeare borrowed from *Woodstock*. Such a hypothesis would explain some of the mysterious references to Woodstock's death in the first act of *Richard II*, since the anonymous play deals with historical events preceding those of Shakespeare's play. Shakespeare's debt to *Jack Straw*, on the other hand, is slight, even though he probably knew the play. Christopher Marlowe's *Edward II* (c. 1592), although dealing with another reign, probably taught Shakespeare much about constructing a play in which a weak king gains sympathy in his suffering while his successor becomes morally tainted by the act of deposition.

Other sources have been proposed, so many in fact that Shakespeare's task of writing the play has been compared to that of a historical researcher. More probably he assimilated his wide and varied reading without any formal program of study. He had certainly read Edward Hall's *Union of the Two Noble Families of Lancaster and York* (1542), a chief source for his earlier history plays, but in *Richard II* he seems to have recalled little more than its overall thematic pattern. Shakespeare must have known the Complaints of Mowbray and Richard in *A Mirror for Magistrates*, but the verbal echoes are slight in this case. The same is essentially true of *The Chronicles of England* by Jean Froissart, translated by Lord Berners (1525), and two French eyewitness accounts available to Shakespeare only in manuscript: the anonymous *Chronique de la Traïson et Mort de Richard Deux Roi d'Angleterre* and Jean Créton's *Histoire du Roi d'Angleterre Richard*. The Froissart *Chronicles* perhaps gave some hints for Gaunt's refusal to avenge Gloucester's death, for Richard's insensitivity at Gaunt's death, and for Northumberland's role as conspirator. The *Traïson* is notably sympathetic to Richard in his decline, although Shakespeare might also have found this sympathy in Daniel's *Civil Wars*.

Shakespeare's second series of English history plays (*Richard II, 1* and *2 Henry IV, Henry V*) is freer of the Tudor providential view of history than was once supposed. The second series does not lead forward by any direct link to the reign of the Tudors, as does the first. Henry A. Kelly has shown (*Divine Providence in the England of Shakespeare's Histories*, 1970), that Shakespeare does not follow a single "Tudor myth" but allows spokesmen for both Richard II and his opponents to repeat arguments found in the various chronicles. This practice is especially evident in *Richard II*, in which some speakers eloquently warn of the disasters that will follow Bolingbroke's assumption of the throne, while other speakers are sympathetic to Bolingbroke's takeover as a political necessity.

THE THIRD VOLUME OF CHRONICLES
(1587 EDITION)

Compiled by Raphael Holinshed

RICHARD THE SECOND

[Holinshed relates the events leading up to the confronta-
tion of Henry, Duke of Hereford, and Thomas Mowbray, Duke
of Norfolk, before King Richard in 1398: Richard's coming to
the throne at the age of eleven in 1377, popular restiveness over
taxes and confused administration, the quarrel between Richard
and his uncle the Duke of Gloucester (Thomas of Woodstock),
Gloucester's plot to imprison and kill King Richard along with
the Dukes of York and Lancaster, the revelation of the plot to
Richard by the Duke of Norfolk, Richard's ordering Norfolk to
kill Gloucester in secret, Norfolk's reluctantly doing so, popular outcry at the death of Gloucester, and uncertainty among
Gloucester's brothers as to how to avenge his death.]

It fell out that, in this Parliament holden at Shrewsbury,
Henry, Duke of Hereford, accused Thomas Mowbray, Duke of
Norfolk, of certain words which he should utter[1] in talk had betwixt them as they rode together lately before[2] betwixt London
and Brentford, sounding highly to the King's dishonor. And for
further proof thereof he presented a supplication to the King
wherein he appealed the Duke of Norfolk in field of battle[3] for a
traitor, false and disloyal to the King and enemy unto the realm.
This supplication was read before both the dukes in presence of
the King; which done, the Duke of Norfolk took upon him to
answer it, declaring that, whatsoever the Duke of Hereford had
said against him other than well, he lied falsely like an untrue
knight as he was. And when the King asked of the Duke of
Hereford what he said to it, he, taking his hood off his head,
said: "My sovereign lord, even as the supplication which I took[4]
you importeth, right so I say for truth, that Thomas Mowbray,

---

1 **should utter** was alleged to have uttered   2 **lately before** recently
3 **appealed . . . battle** i.e., brought an accusation against the Duke of
Norfolk to be tried by combat   4 **took** gave

Duke of Norfolk, is a traitor, false and disloyal to your royal majesty, your crown, and to all the states[5] of your realm."

Then the Duke of Norfolk, being asked what he said to this, he answered: "Right dear lord, with your favor that I make answer unto your cousin here, I say (your reverence saved)[6] that Henry of Lancaster, Duke of Hereford, like a false and disloyal traitor as he is, doth lie in that he hath or shall say of me otherwise than well." "No more," said the King, "we have heard enough"; and herewith commanded the Duke of Surrey, for that turn[7] Marshal of England, to arrest in his name the two dukes. The Duke of Lancaster (father to the Duke of Hereford), the Duke of York, the Duke of Aumerle (Constable of England), and the Duke of Surrey (Marshal of the realm) undertook as pledges, body for body, for the Duke of Hereford; but the Duke of Norfolk was not suffered to put in pledges and so, under arrest, was led unto Windsor Castle and there guarded with keepers that were appointed to see him safely kept.

Now, after the dissolving of the Parliament at Shrewsbury, there was a day appointed about six weeks after for the King to come unto Windsor to hear and to take some order[8] betwixt the two dukes which had thus appealed each other. There was a great scaffold erected within the castle of Windsor for the King to sit with the lords and prelates of his realm; and so, at the day appointed, he with the said lords and prelates being come thither and set in their places, the Duke of Hereford, appellant, and the Duke of Norfolk, defendant, were sent for to come and appear before the King, sitting there in his seat of justice. And then began Sir John Bushy to speak for the King, declaring to the lords how they should understand that where[9] the Duke of Hereford had presented a supplication to the King, who was there set to minister justice to all men that would demand the same, as appertained to his royal majesty, he therefore would

---

5 **states** estates, members of a rank or class of society 6 **your reverence saved** saving your reverence. (An apologetic phrase introducing something that might offend the hearer.) 7 **turn** term, time 8 **take some order** i.e., adjudicate the dispute 9 **where** whereas

now hear what the parties could say one against another; and withal[10] the King commanded the Dukes of Aumerle and Surrey, the one being Constable and the other Marshal, to go unto the two dukes, appellant and defendant, requiring them on his behalf to grow to some agreement; and for his part he would be ready to pardon all that had been said or done amiss betwixt them touching any harm or dishonor to him or his realm. But they answered both assuredly that it was not possible to have any peace or agreement made betwixt them.

When he heard what they had answered, he commanded that they should be brought forthwith before his presence to hear what they would say. Herewith an herald in the King's name, with loud voice, commanded the dukes to come before the King, either[11] of them to show his reason or else to make peace together without more delay. When they were come before the King and lords, the King spake himself to them, willing them to agree and make peace together. "For it is," said he, "the best way ye can take." The Duke of Norfolk, with due reverence, hereunto answered it could not be so brought to pass, his honor saved. Then the King asked of the Duke of Hereford what it was that he demanded of the Duke of Norfolk, "and what is the matter that ye cannot make peace together and become friends?"

Then stood forth a knight who, asking and obtaining license to speak for the Duke of Hereford, said: "Right dear and sovereign lord, here is Henry of Lancaster, Duke of Hereford and Earl of Derby, who saith, and I for him likewise say, that Thomas Mowbray, Duke of Norfolk, is a false and disloyal traitor to you and your royal majesty and to your whole realm; and likewise the Duke of Hereford saith, and I for him, that Thomas Mowbray, Duke of Norfolk, hath received eight thousand nobles to pay the soldiers that keep your town of Calais, which he hath not done as he ought; and furthermore, the said Duke of Norfolk hath been the occasion of all the treason that hath been contrived in your realm for the space of these eighteen years, and by his false suggestions and malicious counsel he

10 withal in addition   11 either each

hath caused to die and to be murdered your right dear uncle, the Duke of Gloucester, son to King Edward. Moreover, the Duke of Hereford saith, and I for him, that he will prove this with his body against the body of the said Duke of Norfolk within lists."[12] The King herewith waxed angry and asked the Duke of Hereford if these were his words, who answered, "Right dear lord, they are my words, and hereof I require right, and the battle against him."

There was a knight also that asked license to speak for the Duke of Norfolk and, obtaining it, began to answer thus: "Right dear sovereign lord, here is Thomas Mowbray, Duke of Norfolk, who answereth and saith, and I for him, that all which Henry of Lancaster hath said and declared, saving the reverence due to the King and his Council, is a lie; and the said Henry of Lancaster hath falsely and wickedly lied as a false and disloyal knight, and both hath been and is a traitor against you, your crown, royal majesty, and realm. This will I prove and defend, as becometh a loyal knight, to do with my body against his. Right dear lord, I beseech you therefore, and your Council, that it may please you in your royal discretion to consider and mark what Henry of Lancaster, Duke of Hereford, such a one as he is, hath said."

The King then demanded of the Duke of Norfolk if these were his words and whether he had any more to say. The Duke of Norfolk then answered for himself: "Right dear sir, true it is that I have received so much gold to pay your people[13] of the town of Calais, which I have done; and I do avouch that your town of Calais is as well kept at your commandment as ever it was at any time before, and that there never hath been by any of Calais any complaint made unto you of me. Right dear and my sovereign lord, for the voyage that I made into France about your marriage, I never received either gold or silver of you, nor yet for the voyage that the Duke of Aumerle and I made into Almaine,[14] where we spent great treasure. Marry, true it is that

12 **within lists** in the place of combat. (The *King Edward* mentioned here is Edward III.)   13 **people** soldiers   14 **Almaine** Germany

once I laid an ambush to have slain the Duke of Lancaster that there sitteth; but nevertheless he hath pardoned me thereof and there was good peace made betwixt us, for the which I yield him hearty thanks. This is that which I have to answer, and I am ready to defend myself against mine adversary. I beseech you therefore of right, and to have the battle against him in upright judgment."

After this, when the King had communed with his Council a little, he commanded the two dukes to stand forth that their answers might be heard. The King then caused them once again to be asked if they would agree and make peace together, but they both flatly answered that they would not; and withal the Duke of Hereford cast down his gage and the Duke of Norfolk took it up. The King, perceiving this demeanor betwixt them, sware by Saint John Baptist that he would never seek to make peace betwixt them again. And therefore Sir John Bushy, in name of the King and his Council, declared that the King and his Council had commanded and ordained that they should have a day of battle appointed them at Coventry. Here writers disagree about the day that was appointed, for some say it was upon a Monday in August, other upon Saint Lambert's Day being the seventeenth of September, other on the eleventh of September; but true it is that the King assigned them not only the day but also appointed them lists and place for the combat, and thereupon great preparation was made as to such a matter appertained.

At the time appointed the King came to Coventry, where the two dukes were ready according to the order prescribed therein, coming thither in great array accompanied with the lords and gentlemen of their lineages.[15] The King caused a sumptuous scaffold or theater and royal lists there to be erected and prepared. The Sunday before they should fight, after dinner, the Duke of Hereford came to the King (being lodged about a quarter of a mile without the town in a tower that belonged to Sir William Bagot) to take his leave of him. The morrow after,

15 lineages retinues.

being the day appointed for the combat, about the spring of the day[16] came the Duke of Norfolk to the court to take leave likewise of the King. The Duke of Hereford armed him in his tent, that was set up near to the lists, and the Duke of Norfolk put on his armor betwixt the gate and the barrier of the town, in a beautiful house having a fair parclose[17] of wood towards the gate that none might see what was done within the house.

The Duke of Aumerle, that day being High Constable of England, and the Duke of Surrey, Marshal, placed themselves betwixt them, well armed and appointed; and when they saw their time, they first entered into the lists with a great company of men appareled in silk sendal[18] embroidered with silver both richly and curiously,[19] every man having a tipped staff to keep the field in order. About the hour of prime[20] came to the barriers of the lists the Duke of Hereford, mounted on a white courser barded[21] with green and blue velvet embroidered sumptuously with swans and antelopes of goldsmith's work, armed at all points. The Constable and Marshal came to the barriers, demanding of him what he was. He answered: "I am Henry of Lancaster, Duke of Hereford, which am come hither to do mine endeavor against Thomas Mowbray, Duke of Norfolk, as a traitor untrue to God, the King, his realm, and me." Then incontinently[22] he sware upon the holy evangelists that his quarrel was true and just, and upon that point he required[23] to enter the lists. Then he put up his sword, which before he held naked in his hand, and, putting down his visor, made a cross on his horse, and with spear in hand entered into the lists and descended from his horse and set him down in a chair of green velvet at the one end of the lists and there reposed himself, abiding the coming of his adversary.

Soon after him entered into the field with great triumph King Richard, accompanied with all the peers of the realm; and

16 **the spring of the day** early morning   17 **parclose** partition, screen 18 **sendal** a thin, rich material   19 **curiously** delicately   20 **prime** 9 A.M.   21 **barded** caparisoned, richly covered 22 **incontinently** immediately   23 **required** asked permission

in his company was the Earl of Saint-Pol, which was come out of France in post[24] to see this challenge performed. The King had there above ten thousand men in armor, lest some fray or tumult might rise amongst his nobles by quarreling or partaking.[25] When the King was set in his seat, which was richly hanged and adorned, a king at arms[26] made open proclamation prohibiting all men, in the name of the King and of the High Constable and Marshal, to enterprise or attempt to approach or touch any part of the lists upon pain of death, except such as were appointed to order or marshal the field. The proclamation ended, another herald cried: "Behold here Henry of Lancaster, Duke of Hereford, appellant, which is entered into the lists royal to do his devoir[27] against Thomas Mowbray, Duke of Norfolk, defendant, upon pain to be found false and recreant!"

The Duke of Norfolk hovered on horseback at the entry of the lists, his horse being barded with crimson velvet embroidered richly with lions of silver and mulberry trees; and when he had made his oath before the Constable and Marshal that his quarrel was just and true, he entered the field manfully, saying aloud, "God aid him that hath the right!"; and then he departed from his horse and sat him down in his chair, which was of crimson velvet curtained about with white and red damask. The Lord Marshal viewed their spears to see that they were of equal length and delivered the one spear himself to the Duke of Hereford and sent the other unto the Duke of Norfolk by a knight. Then the herald proclaimed that the traverses[28] and chairs of the champions should be removed, commanding them on the King's behalf to mount on horseback and address themselves to the battle and combat.

The Duke of Hereford was quickly horsed, and closed his beaver and cast his spear into the rest,[29] and when the trumpet sounded set forward courageously towards his enemy six or seven paces. The Duke of Norfolk was not fully set forward

24 **in post** in haste   25 **partaking** taking sides.   26 **king at arms** chief herald   27 **devoir** appointed task, utmost   28 **traverses** curtained compartments   29 **rest** resting place for the base of the spear

when the King cast down his warder[30] and the heralds cried, "Ho, ho!" Then the King caused their spears to be taken from them and commanded them to repair again to their chairs, where they remained two long hours while the King and his Council deliberately consulted what order was best to be had in so weighty a cause. Finally, after they had devised and fully determined what should be done therein, the heralds cried silence, and Sir John Bushy, the King's secretary, read the sentence and determination of the King and his Council in a long roll, the effect whereof was that Henry, Duke of Hereford, should within fifteen days depart out of the realm and not to return before the term of ten years were expired except[31] by the King he should be repealed[32] again, and this upon pain of death; and that Thomas Mowbray, Duke of Norfolk, because he had sown sedition in the realm by his words, should likewise avoid the realm and never to return again into England nor approach the borders or confines thereof upon pain of death; and that the King would stay[33] the profits of his[34] lands till he had levied thereof such sums of money as the Duke had taken up of the King's treasurer for the wages of the garrison of Calais which were still unpaid.

When these judgments were once read, the King called before him both the parties and made them to swear that the one should never come in place where the other was, willingly, nor keep any company together in any foreign region; which oath they both received humbly and so went their ways. The Duke of Norfolk departed sorrowfully out of the realm into Almaine and at the last came to Venice, where he for thought[35] and melancholy deceased; for he was in hope (as writers record) that he should have been borne out[36] in the matter by the King, which when it fell out otherwise it grieved him not a little. The Duke of Hereford took his leave of the King at Eltham, who there released four years of his banishment; so he took his journey over into Calais and from thence went into France, where he re-

30 **warder** baton   31 **except** unless   32 **repealed** recalled   33 **stay** detain, hold back   34 **his** i.e., Mowbray's   35 **thought** sorrow   36 **borne out** backed, supported

mained. A wonder it was to see what number of people ran after him in every town and street where he came before he took the sea, lamenting and bewailing his departure, as who would say[37] that when he departed, the only shield, defense, and comfort of the commonwealth was vaded[38] and gone.

[The Duke of Hereford is well received by the French King Charles the Sixth, who proposes a marriage treaty until the matter is blocked by King Richard's ambassadors.]

But yet, to content the King's[39] mind, many blank charters[40] were devised and brought into the City,[41] which many of the substantial and wealthy citizens were fain[42] to seal, to their great charge,[43] as in the end appeared. And the like charters were sent abroad into all shires within the realm, whereby great grudge and murmuring arose among the people; for when they were so sealed, the King's officers wrote in the same what liked them,[44] as well for charging the parties with payment of money as otherwise.

In this meantime the Duke of Lancaster[45] departed out of this life at the Bishop of Ely's place in Holborn and lieth buried in the cathedral church of Saint Paul in London, on the north side of the high altar, by the Lady Blanche his first wife. The death of this Duke gave occasion of increasing more hatred in the people of this realm toward the King, for he seized into his hands all the goods that belonged to him and also received all the rents and revenues of his lands which ought to have descended unto the Duke of Hereford by lawful inheritance, in revoking

---

37 as who would say as one might say   **38 vaded** departed   **39 the King's** i.e., Richard's   **40 blank charters** writs authorizing the collection of revenues or forced loans to the crown, with blank spaces being left for the collectors to fill in the name of the payer and the amount he must pay; see *Richard II*, 1.4.48   **41 the City** i.e., London   **42 fain** obliged   **43 charge** expense   **44 liked them** they pleased   **45 the Duke of Lancaster** John of Gaunt, who died in February 1399

his letters patents,[46] which he had granted to him before, by virtue whereof he might make his attorneys general to sue livery[47] for him, of any manner of inheritances or possessions that might from thenceforth fall unto him, and that his homage might be respited with making reasonable fine.[48] Whereby it was evident that the King meant his utter undoing.

This hard dealing was much misliked of[49] all the nobility and cried out against of the meaner sort;[50] but namely[51] the Duke of York was therewith sore moved, who, before this time, had borne things with so patient a mind as he could, though the same touched him very near, as[52] the death of his brother the Duke of Gloucester, the banishment of his nephew the said Duke of Hereford, and other more injuries in great number which, for[53] the slippery youth of the King, he passed over for the time and did forget as well as he might. But now, perceiving that neither law, justice, nor equity could take place where the King's willful will was bent upon any wrongful purpose, he considered that the glory of the public wealth[54] of his country must needs decay by reason of the King his[55] lack of wit and want of such as would without flattery admonish him of his duty; and therefore he thought it the part of a wise man to get him in time to a resting place and to leave the following of such an unadvised captain[56] as with a leaden sword would cut his own throat.

Hereupon he, with the Duke of Aumerle his son, went to his house at Langley, rejoicing that nothing had mishappened in the commonwealth through his device or consent. The com-

---

46 letters patents royal grant giving the privilege to sue through one's attorneys for possession of one's inheritance; see *Richard II*, 2.1.202 **47 sue livery** sue for possession of hereditary rights; see previous note and *Richard II*, 2.3.129 **48 that . . . fine** that the formal acknowledgment of allegiance under the feudal system which was incumbent upon him might be postponed by means of his paying a reasonable fine. **49 misliked of** disliked by **50 of the meaner sort** by those of lower station **51 namely** especially **52 as** such as **53 for** taking into account **54 public wealth** common welfare **55 King his** King's **56 unadvised captain** ill-advised ruler

mon bruit[57] ran that the King had set to farm the realm of England unto Sir William Scroop, Earl of Wiltshire and then Treasurer of England, to Sir John Bushy, Sir John Bagot, and Sir Henry Green, knights. About the same time, the Earl of Arundel's son, named Thomas, which was kept in the Duke of Exeter's house, escaped out of the realm by means of one William Scott, mercer, and went to his uncle, Thomas Arundel, late Archbishop of Canterbury, as then sojourning at Cologne.

King Richard, being destitute of treasure to furnish such a princely port as he maintained, borrowed great sums of money of many of the great lords and peers of his realm, both spiritual and temporal, and likewise of other mean persons, promising them in good earnest by delivering to them his letters patents for assurance that he would repay the money so borrowed at a day appointed, which notwithstanding he never paid. . . .

In this year, in a manner throughout all the realm of England, old bay trees withered and afterwards, contrary to all men's thinking, grew green again—a strange sight and supposed to import some unknown event. In this meantime the King, being advertised that the wild Irish daily wasted and destroyed the towns and villages within the English Pale[58] and had slain many of the soldiers which lay there in garrison for defense of that country, determined to make eftsoons[59] a voyage thither and prepared all things necessary for his passage now against the spring.[60] A little before his setting forth, he caused a jousts to be holden at Windsor of forty knights and forty esquires against all comers, and they to be appareled in green, with a white falcon, and the Queen[61] to be there well accompanied with ladies and damsels. When these jousts were finished, the King departed toward Bristol, from thence to pass into Ireland, leaving the Queen with her train still at Windsor. He appointed for his lieutenant general in his absence his uncle the Duke of York. And

---

57 bruit rumor   **58 the English Pale** the area under English jurisdiction. (The year is 1399.)   **59 eftsoons** again   **60 against the spring** in anticipation of the coming of spring.   **61 the Queen** i.e., Isabella (then aged twelve), Richard's second wife

so, in the month of April, as divers authors write, he set forward from Windsor and finally took shipping at Milford, and from thence with two hundred ships and a puissant power of men-of-arms and archers he sailed into Ireland. . . .

Now whilst he was thus occupied in devising how to reduce them[62] into subjection, and taking orders for the good stay and quiet government of the country, divers of the nobility, as well prelates as other, and likewise many of the magistrates and rulers of the cities, towns, and commonalty here in England, perceiving daily how the realm drew to utter ruin, not like[63] to be recovered to the former state of wealth whilst King Richard lived and reigned (as they took it), devised with great deliberation and considerate advice, to send and signify by letters unto Duke Henry, whom they now called (as he was indeed) Duke of Lancaster and Hereford, requiring him with all convenient speed to convey himself into England, promising him all their aid, power, and assistance if he, expelling King Richard as a man not meet for the office he bare, would take upon him the scepter, rule, and diadem of his native land and region.

[Duke Henry readies a fleet at Le Port Blanc in Brittany and sails for England in the company of Thomas Arundel, Archbishop of Canterbury, and others.]

When the Lord Governor, Edmund, Duke of York, was advertised[64] that the Duke of Lancaster kept still the sea and was ready to arrive (but where he meant first to set foot on land there was not any that understood the certainty), he sent for the Lord Chancellor, Edmund Stafford, Bishop of Exeter, and for the Lord Treasurer, William Scoop, Earl of Wiltshire, and other of the King's Privy Council, as John Bushy, William Bagot, Henry Green, and John Russell, knights. Of these he required to know what they thought good to be done in this matter concerning the Duke of Lancaster being on the seas. Their advice

62 them i.e., the Irish   **63 like** likely   **64 advertised** advised, informed

was to depart from London unto Saint Albans and there to
gather an army to resist the Duke in his landing; but to how
small purpose their counsel served, the conclusion thereof
plainly declared. For the most part that[65] were called, when they
came thither, boldly protested that they would not fight against
the Duke of Lancaster whom they knew to be evil dealt withal.

The Lord Treasurer, Bushy, Bagot, and Green, perceiving
that the commons would cleave unto and take part with the
Duke, slipped away, leaving the Lord Governor of the realm and
the Lord Chancellor to make what shift they could for themselves. Bagot got him to Chester and so escaped into Ireland; the
other fled to the castle of Bristol in hope there to be in safety.
The Duke of Lancaster, after that he had coasted alongst the
shore a certain time and had got some intelligence how the people's minds were affected towards him, landed about the beginning of July[66] in Yorkshire, at a place sometime[67] called Ravenspur,
betwixt Hull and Bridlington, and with him not past threescore
persons, as some write; but he was so joyfully received of the
lords, knights, and gentlemen of those parts that he found
means (by their help) forthwith to assemble a great number of
people that were willing to take his part. The first that came to
him were the lords of Lincolnshire and other countries adjoin-
ing, as the Lords Willoughby, Ross, Darcy, and Beaumont.

At his coming unto Doncaster, the Earl of Northumberland
and his son Sir Henry Percy, Wardens of the Marches against
Scotland, with the Earl of Westmorland, came unto him, where
he sware unto those lords that he would demand no more but
the lands that were to him descended by inheritance from his
father and in right of his wife. Moreover, he undertook to cause
the payment of taxes and tallages[68] to be laid down, and to bring
the King to good government, and to remove from him the
Cheshire men, which were envied of[69] many; for that the King
esteemed of them more than of any other, haply because they

65 the most part that most of those who   66 July i.e., in 1399
67 sometime formerly   68 tallages levies, taxes   69 envied of re-
sented by

were more faithful to him than other, ready in all respects to obey his commandments and pleasure. From Doncaster, having now got a mighty army about him, he marched forth with all speed through the countries, coming by Evesham unto Berkeley. Within the space of three days all the King's castles in those parts were surrendered unto him.

[The Duke of York, unable to resist, goes over to Duke Henry's side. Sir Henry Green, Sir John Bushy, and the Lord William Scroop, Earl of Wiltshire, are taken and executed. Richard is delayed in returning from Ireland by contrary winds. He arrives at last near Barkloughly Castle in Wales, only to learn that the Welsh have already given up his cause, that his trusty counselors have been executed, and that most of the nation is against him. "He became so greatly discomforted that, sorrowfully lamenting his miserable state, he utterly despaired of his own safety and, calling his army together, which was not small, licensed every man to depart to his home." Sir Thomas Percy, Earl of Worcester, Lord Steward of the King's household, breaks his staff of office and joins Duke Henry. Richard takes refuge in Flint Castle, where he agrees to a parley with Duke Henry and his allies, is ambushed by the Earl of Northumberland and his men, and at last confronts his challenger.]

The King, that was walking aloft on the brayes[70] of the walls to behold the coming of the Duke[71] afar off, might see that the Archbishop[72] and the other were come and, as he took it, to talk with him. Whereupon he forthwith came down unto them, and beholding that they did their due reverence to him on their knees, he took them up and, drawing the Archbishop aside from the residue, talked with him a good while; and as it was reported, the Archbishop willed him to be of good comfort, for he should be assured not to have any hurt as touching his person;

70 brayes parapets **71 the Duke** i.e., the Duke of Hereford (Bolingbroke)   **72 the Archbishop** i.e., the Archbishop of Canterbury

but he prophesied not as a prelate but as a Pilate.[73] For was it no hurt, think you, to his person to be spoiled of his royalty, to be deposed from his crown, to be translated from principality to prison, and to fall from honor into horror? All which befell him to his extreme heart grief, no doubt, which to increase, means alas there were many, but to diminish, helps, God wot, but a few. . . .

After that the Archbishop had now here at Flint communed with the King, he departed and, taking his horse again, rode back to meet the Duke, who began at that present[74] to approach the castle and compassed it round about, even down to the sea, with his people, ranged in good and seemly order at the foot of the mountains. And then the Earl of Northumberland, passing forth of the castle to the Duke, talked with him awhile in sight of the King, being again got up to the walls to take better view of the army, being now advanced within two bowshots of the castle, to the small rejoicing (ye may be sure) of the sorrowful King. The Earl of Northumberland, returning to the castle, appointed the King to be set to dinner (for he was fasting till then); and after he had dined, the Duke came down to the castle himself and entered the same all armed, his basinet[75] only excepted; and being within the first gate, he stayed there till the King came forth of the inner part of the castle unto him.

The King, accompanied with the Bishop of Carlisle, the Earl of Salisbury, and Sir Stephen Scroop, knight, who bare the sword before him, and a few other, came forth into the utter ward[76] and sat down in a place prepared for him. Forthwith, as the Duke got sight of the King, he showed a reverent duty as became him in bowing his knee, and coming forward did so likewise the second and third time, till the King took him by the hand and lift him up, saying, "Dear cousin, ye are welcome." The Duke, humbly thanking him, said: "My sovereign lord and king, the cause of

73 **Pilate** i.e., one washing his hands of the business (as Pontius Pilate attempted to do with the crucifixion of Christ).   74 **at that present** at that time   75 **basinet** steel headpiece   76 **utter ward** outer circuit of the walls of the castle

my coming at this present is (your honor saved) to have again restitution of my person, my lands, and heritage through your favorable license." The King hereunto answered: "Dear cousin, I am ready to accomplish your will so that ye may enjoy all that is yours without exception."

Meeting thus together, they came forth of the castle and the King there called for wine; and after they had drunk they mounted on horseback and rode that night to Flint and so the next day unto Chester . . . and so came to London. Neither was the King permitted all this while to change his apparel, but rode still through all these towns simply clothed in one suit of raiment, and yet he was in his time exceeding sumptuous in apparel, insomuch as he had one coat which he caused to be made for him of gold and stone valued at 30,000 marks. And so he was brought the next way to Westminster.

As for the Duke, he was received with all the joy and pomp that might be of the Londoners and was lodged in the Bishop's palace by Paul's Church. It was a wonder to see what great concourse of people and what number of horses came to him on the way as he thus passed the countries, till his coming to London, where, upon his approach to the city, the Mayor rode forth to receive him, and a great number of other citizens. Also the clergy met him with procession; and such joy appeared in the countenances of the people, uttering the same also with words, as the like not lightly been seen.[77] For in every town and village where he passed children rejoiced, women clapped their hands, and men cried out for joy. But to speak of the great numbers of people that flocked together in the fields and streets of London at his coming I here omit; neither will I speak of the presents, welcomings, lauds, and gratifications made to him by the citizens and commonalty.

But now to the purpose. The next day after his coming to London, the King from Westminster was had to the Tower and there committed to safe custody. Many evil-disposed persons, assembling themselves together in great numbers, intended to have met with him and to have taken him from such as had the

77 **as . . . seen** such as had not commonly been seen.

conveying of him, that they might have slain him. But the Mayor and aldermen gathered to them the worshipful commoners and grave citizens, by whose policy, and not without much ado, the other were revoked from their evil purpose. . . .

After this was a Parliament called by the Duke of Lancaster, using the name of King Richard in the writs directed forth to the lords and other states for their summons. This Parliament began the thirteenth day of September, in the which many heinous points of misgovernance and injurious dealings in the administration of his kingly office were laid to the charge of this noble prince, King Richard.

[Thirty-three articles are brought against Richard, detailing the reasons for which he is accounted worthy to be deposed. The delicate matter of persuading Richard to agree to the deposition is entrusted to certain followers of his who have access to his person. They exhort him to save his life by thus agreeing.]

And first they advised him willingly to suffer himself to be deposed and to resign his right of his own accord, so that the Duke of Lancaster might without murder or battle obtain the scepter and diadem, after which, they well perceived, he gaped; by means whereof they thought he[78] might be in perfect assurance of his life long to continue. Whether this their persuasion proceeded by the suborning of the Duke of Lancaster and his favorers, or of a sincere affection which they bare to the King as supposing it most sure in such an extremity, it is uncertain; but yet the effect followed not,[79] howsoever their meaning was. Notwithstanding, the King, being now in the hands of his enemies and utterly despairing of all comfort, was easily persuaded to renounce his crown and princely preeminence, so that, in hope of life only, he agreed to all things that were of him demanded. And so (as it should seem by the copy of an instrument hereafter

78 he i.e., Richard. (The date is September 1399.)   **79 the effect followed not** i.e., Richard's life was not saved by this means

following) he renounced and voluntarily was deposed from his royal crown and kingly dignity, the Monday being the nine-and-twentieth day of September and feast of Saint Michael the Archangel, in the year of our Lord 1399 and in three-and-twentieth year of his reign. The copy of which instrument here ensueth.

[Holinshed here prints "a copy of the instrument touching the declaration of the commissioners sent from the states in Parliament unto King Richard," followed by "the tenor of the instrument whereby King Richard resigneth the crown to the Duke of Lancaster."]

"In the name of God, amen. I, Richard, by the grace of God King of England and of France, etc., Lord of Ireland, acquit and assoil[80] all archbishops, bishops, and other prelates, secular or religious, of what dignity, degree, state, or condition soever they be, and also all dukes, marquesses, earls, barons, lords, and all my liege men, both spiritual and secular, of what manner or degree they be, from their oath of fealty and homage and all other deeds and privileges made unto me, and from all manner bonds of allegiance, regality, and lordship in which they were or be bounden to me or any otherwise constrained; and them, their heirs, and successors forevermore from the same bonds and oaths I release, deliver, and acquit and set them for free, dissolved and acquit, and to be harmless, forasmuch as longeth[81] to my person by any manner way or title of right that to me might follow of the foresaid things, or any of them. And also I resign all my kingly dignity, majesty, and crown, with all the lordships, power, and privileges to the foresaid kingly dignity and crown belonging, and all other lordships and possessions to me in any manner of wise pertaining, of what name, title, quality, or condition soever they be, except the lands and possessions for me and mine obits[82] purchased and bought. And I renounce all right and all manner of title of possession which I ever had or

80 **assoil** absolve   81 **longeth** belongs   82 **obits** ceremonies performed in behalf of the soul of the deceased

have in the same lordships and possessions, or any of them, with any manner of rights belonging or appertaining unto any part of them. . . ."

[The King, in the presence of the commissioners, subscribes to this document and delivers it to the Archbishop of Canterbury,]

saying that, if it were in his power or at his assignment, he would that the Duke of Lancaster there present should be his successor and king after him. And in token hereof he took a ring of gold from his finger, being his signet, and put it upon the said Duke's finger, desiring and requiring the Archbishop of York and the Bishop of Hereford to show and make report unto the lords of the Parliament of his voluntary resignation and also of his intent and good mind that he bare towards his cousin the Duke of Lancaster to have him his successor and their king after him. All this done, every man took their leave and returned to their own.

Upon the morrow after, being Tuesday and the last day of September, all the lords spiritual and temporal with the commons of the said Parliament assembled at Westminster where, in the presence of them, the Archbishop of York and the Bishop of Hereford, according to the King's request, showed unto them the voluntary renouncing of the King with the favor also which he bare to his cousin of Lancaster to have him his successor; and moreover showed them the schedule or bill of renouncement signed with King Richard's own hand, which they caused to be read first in Latin, as it was written, and after in English. This done, the question was first asked of the lords if they would admit and allow that renouncement; the which, when it was of them granted and confirmed, the like question was asked of the commons and of them in like manner confirmed. After this, it was then declared that notwithstanding the foresaid renouncing, so by the lords and commons admitted and confirmed, it were necessary, in avoiding of all suspicions and surmises of evil-disposed persons, to have in writing and registered the manifold crimes and defaults before done by King Richard to the end that they might first be openly declared to the people and after to remain of record amongst other of the King's records forever.

All thus was done accordingly, for the articles which before ye have heard were drawn and engrossed up and there ready to be read; but for other causes more needful as then to be preferred, the reading of those articles at that season was deferred. Then, forsomuch as the lords of the Parliament had well considered the voluntary resignation of King Richard and that it was behooveful and, as they thought, necessary for the weal of the realm to proceed unto the sentence of his deposing, there were appointed, by the authority of all the estates there in Parliament assembled, the Bishop of Saint Asaph, the Abbot of Glastonbury, the Earl of Gloucester, the Lord Berkeley, William Thirning, Justice, and Thomas Erpingham with Thomas Grey, knights, that they should give and pronounce the open sentence of the deposing of King Richard.

[Holinshed here prints "the publication of King Richard's deposing," in which the commissioners declare their purpose to deprive Richard "of all kingly dignity and worship and of any kingly worship in himself. And we depose him by our sentence definitive," expressly forbidding all prelates, nobles, and commoners of the realm to offer Richard any obedience.]

Immediately as the sentence was in this wise passed, and that by reason thereof the realm stood void without head or governor for the time, the Duke of Lancaster, rising from the place where before he sat and standing where all those in the house might behold him, in reverent manner made a sign of the cross on his forehead and likewise on his breast and, after silence by an officer commanded, said unto the people there being present these words following:

"In the name of the Father, and of the Son, and of the Holy Ghost, I, Henry of Lancaster, claim the realm of England and the crown, with all the appurtenances, as I that am descended by right line of the blood coming from that good Lord King Henry the Third, and through the right that God of His grace hath sent me, with the help of my kin and of my friends, to recover the same, which was in point to be undone for default of good governance and due justice."

After these words thus by him uttered, he returned and sat him down in the place where before he had sitten. Then the lords, having heard and well perceived this claim thus made by this nobleman, each of them asked of other what they thought therein. At length, after a little pausing or stay made, the Archbishop of Canterbury, having notice of the minds of the lords, stood up and asked the commons if they would assent to the lords, which in their minds thought the claim of the Duke made to be rightful and necessary for the wealth of the realm and them all; whereto the commons with one voice cried, "Yea, yea, yea!" After which answer the said Archbishop, going to the Duke and kneeling down before him on his knee, addressed to him all his purpose in few words. The which when he had ended, he rose and, taking the Duke by the right hand, led him unto the King's seat, the Archbishop of York assisting him, and with great reverence set him therein, after that the Duke had first upon his knees made his prayer in devout manner unto almighty God.

[The Archbishop of Canterbury delivers a sermon in honor of Henry IV's accession, to which the King replies. October 13 is proclaimed as the solemn day of King Henry's coronation.]

Thus was King Richard deprived of all kingly honor and princely dignity, by reason he was so given to follow evil counsel, and used such inconvenient[83] ways and means, through insolent misgovernance and youthful outrage, though otherwise a right noble and worthy prince. He reigned two-and-twenty years, three months, and eight days. He delivered to King Henry, now that he was thus deposed, all the goods that he had, to the sum of three hundred thousand pounds in coin, besides plate and jewels, as a pledge and satisfaction of the injuries by him committed and done, in hope to be in more surety of life for the

83 **inconvenient** improper

delivery thereof. But, whatsoever was promised, he was deceived therein. For shortly after his resignation he was conveyed to the castle of Leeds in Kent, and from thence to Pomfret, where he departed out of this miserable life, as after you shall hear. He was seemly of shape and favor, and of nature good enough if the wickedness and naughty demeanor of such as were about him had not altered it.

His chance[84] verily was greatly infortunate, which fell into such calamity that he took it for the best way he could devise to renounce his kingdom, for the which mortal men are accustomed to hazard all they have to attain thereunto. But such misfortune (or the like) oftentimes falleth unto those princes which, when they are aloft, cast no doubt[85] for perils that may follow. He was prodigal, ambitious, and much given to the pleasure of the body. He kept the greatest port[86] and maintained the most plentiful house that ever any king in England did either before his time or since. For there resorted daily to his court above ten thousand persons that had meat and drink there allowed them. In his kitchen there were three hundred servitors, and every other office was furnished after the like rate. Of ladies, chamberers, and launderers, there were above three hundred at the least. And in gorgeous and costly apparel they exceeded all measure, not one of them that kept within the bounds of his degree. Yeomen and grooms were clothed in silks, with cloth of grain[87] and scarlet, oversumptuous ye may be sure for their estates. And this vanity was not only used in the court in those days but also other people abroad in the towns and countries had their garments cut far otherwise than had been accustomed before his days, with embroideries, rich furs, and goldsmith's work, and every day there was devising of new fashions, to the great hindrance and decay of the commonwealth.

Moreover, such were preferred to bishoprics and other ecclesiastical livings as neither could teach nor preach nor knew any

---

84 chance fortune   **85 aloft, cast no doubt** i.e., prosperous and high on Fortune's wheel, show no concern, make no provision   **86 port** style of living   **87 grain** purple

thing of the scripture of God but only to call for their tithes and duties; so that they were most unworthy the name of bishops, being lewd[88] and most vain persons disguised in bishops' apparel. Furthermore, there reigned abundantly the filthy sin of lechery and fornication, with abominable adultery, specially in the King but most chiefly in the prelacy, whereby the whole realm by such their evil example was so infected that the wrath of God was daily provoked to vengeance for the sins of the prince and his people. . . .

Thus have ye heard what writers do report touching the state of the time and doings of this King. But if I may boldly say what I think, he was a prince the most unthankfully used of his subjects of any one of whom ye shall lightly read. For although, through the frailty of youth, he demeaned himself more dissolutely than seemed convenient for his royal estate and made choice of such councillors as were not favored by the people, whereby he was the less favored himself, yet in no king's days were the commons in greater wealth, if they could have perceived their happy state, neither in any other time were the nobles and gentlemen more cherished, nor churchmen less wronged. But such was their ingratitude towards their bountiful and loving sovereign that those whom he had chiefly advanced were readiest to control him; for that they might not rule all things at their will, and remove from him such as they misliked, and place in their rooms whom they thought good, and that rather by strong hand than by gentle and courteous means, which stirred such malice betwixt him and them, till at length it could not be assuaged without peril of destruction to them both.

[Accusations are brought against those thought to be guilty of the Duke of Gloucester's death and especially against the Duke of Aumerle. Many throw down their gages against him. News arrives of the deaths of the Duke of Norfolk in Venice and of the Duchess of Gloucester. The Abbot of Westminster is involved in a conspiracy against King Henry IV, and the Duke of

88 lewd ignorant

York rides hastily to Windsor to accuse his own son the Earl of Rutland (i.e., Aumerle) of plotting against the throne. The Abbot of Westminster commits suicide; the Bishop of Carlisle is pardoned.]

And immediately after, King Henry, to rid himself of any suchlike danger to be attempted against him thereafter, caused King Richard to die of a violent death, that no man should afterward feign himself to represent his person, though some have said he was not privy to that wicked offense.

[Various reports attribute Richard's death to forced starvation or to voluntary pining away.]

One writer,[89] which seemeth to have great knowledge of King Richard's doings, saith that King Henry, sitting on a day at his table, sore sighing, said: "Have I no faithful friend which will deliver me of him whose life will be my death and whose death will be the preservation of my life?" This saying was much noted of them which were present and especially of one called Sir Piers of Exton. This knight incontinently[90] departed from the court with eight strong persons in his company and came to Pomfret, commanding the esquire that was accustomed to sew[91] and take the assay[92] before King Richard to do so no more, saying, "Let him eat now, for he shall not long eat." King Richard sat down to dinner and was served without courtesy or assay, whereupon, much marveling at the sudden change, he demanded of the esquire why he did not his duty. "Sir," said he, "I am otherwise commanded by Sir Piers of Exton, which is newly come from King Henry." When King Richard heard that word, he took the carving knife in his hand and strake[93] the esquire on the head, saying, "The devil take Henry of Lancaster and thee together!" And with that word Sir Piers entered the chamber,

89 One writer i.e., Thomas of Walsingham   90 incontinently immediately. (The date is February 1400.)   91 sew serve food   92 take the assay i.e., taste the food before the King eats   93 strake struck

well armed, with eight tall[94] men likewise armed, every of them having a bill[95] in his hand.

King Richard, perceiving this, put the table from him and, stepping to the foremost man, wrung the bill out of his hands and so valiantly defended himself that he slew four of those that thus came to assail him. Sir Piers, being half dismayed herewith, leaped into the chair where King Richard was wont to sit, while the other four persons fought with him and chased him about the chamber. And in conclusion, as King Richard traversed his ground from one side of the chamber to another, and coming by the chair where Sir Piers stood, he was felled with a stroke of a poleax which Sir Piers gave him upon the head, and therewith rid him out of life without giving him respite once to call to God for mercy of his past offenses. It is said that Sir Piers of Exton, after he had thus slain him, wept right bitterly, as one stricken with the prick of a guilty conscience, for murdering him whom he had so long time obeyed as king. After he was thus dead, his body was embalmed and cered[96] and covered with lead, all save the face, to the intent that all men might see him and perceive that he was departed this life; for as the corpse was conveyed from Pomfret to London, in all the towns and places where those that had the conveyance of it did stay with it all night, they caused dirige[97] to be sung in the evening and mass of requiem in the morning; and as well after the one service as the other, his face discovered was showed to all that coveted to behold it.

Thus was the corpse first brought to the Tower and, after, through the City to the cathedral church of Saint Paul, barefaced, where it lay three days together that all men might behold it. There was a solemn obsequy done for him, both at Paul's and after at Westminster, at which time, both at dirige overnight and in the morning at the mass of requiem, the King and the citi-

---

94 tall bold, doughty   **95 bill** long-handled, axlike weapon; halberd
96 cered wrapped in a cerecloth or waxed winding-sheet   **97 dirige**
(The Office of the Dead in the Roman Catholic Church, based on
Psalm 5.)

zens of London were present. When the same was ended, the corpse was commanded to be had unto Langley, there to be buried in the church of the Friars Preachers. . . . He was after by King Henry the Fifth removed to Westminster and there honorably entombed with Queen Anne[98] his wife.

98 Anne Anne of Bohemia, Richard's first wife

The second edition of Raphael Holinshed's *Chronicles* was published in 1587. These selections are based on that edition, Volume 3, pages 493–517.

FURTHER READING

Barkan, Leonard. "The Theatrical Consistency of *Richard II*." *Shakespeare Quarterly* 29 (1978): 5–19. Barkan examines the "emotional texture" of the play, finding that the "suppressed passion" of the first half is "balanced and resolved" in the fourth and fifth acts by "a series of explosive releases." With Richard's removal from power, the passionate energies, no longer contained, transform England and the play itself from worlds of ritual to worlds where violence is real.

Berger, Harry, Jr. "Textual Dramaturgy: Representing the Limits of Theatre in *Richard II*." *Theatre Journal* 39 (1987): 135–55. Berger explores the self-conscious theatricality of the characters as it is used as a strategy of "repression and displacement." Focusing especially on the episode of Aumerle and York as a caricature of the relationship of Bolingbroke and Gaunt, Berger finds it emblematic of a play that reveals public display as an effort of misdirection, deflecting attention from the real issues of the "psychopolitical drama."

Blank, Paula. "Speaking Freely about Richard II." *Journal of English and Germanic Philology* 96 (1997): 327–48. Starting from the fact of the first three quartos' notorious omission of the deposition scene, Blank interestingly examines the play's concerns with self-censorship as it explores the very nature of royal power. Blank uses the two central meanings of the word "deposition" (the removal of a king from power and the testimony formally taken in trial) to show how the play explores the vexed issue of "free speech" as part of its account of how political power is both established and resisted.

Bolam, Robin. "*Richard II*: Shakespeare and the Languages of the Stage." *Cambridge Companion to Shakespeare's History Plays*, ed. Michael Hattaway. Cambridge: Cambridge Univ. Press, 2002. In a subtle reading of the play focusing on its own structures of imagery, its performance history, and its original historical context, Bolam recognizes the various "languages" of *Richard II*, its different registers and styles, as well as the play's own self-consciousness about language itself (of all Shakespeare's plays, it has the "highest proportion of key words concerning language"). For Bolam the often confusing political action of the play uses words, silences, spectacle, and gesture "to create drama" that is fundamentally "about language—its power and weaknesses."

Campbell, Lily B. "An Introduction into the Division Between Lancaster and York." *Shakespeare's "Histories": Mirrors of Elizabethan Policy.* San Marino, Calif.: Huntington Library, 1947. Using Elizabethan chronicles, political pamphlets, and other sixteenth-century texts, Campbell establishes the relationship between the historical events depicted in *Richard II* and the political concerns of Elizabethan England.

Coleridge, Samuel Taylor. *"Richard II." Coleridge's Writings on Shakespeare,* ed. Terence Hawkes. New York: G. P. Putnam's Sons, 1959. *Richard II,* the most "purely historical" of Shakespeare's plays, is seen by Coleridge as exploring "the vast importance of the personal character of the sovereign." Richard is seen to be "weak, variable, and womanish," sheltering himself from reality "by a cloud of his own thoughts." Bolingbroke is a man of ambition, encouraged by his grievances and those of his country, but "at the same time scarcely daring to look at his own views, or to acknowledge them as designs."

Farrell, Kirby, ed. *Critical Essays on Shakespeare's "Richard II."* New York: G. K. Hall, 1999. A useful selection of essays on the play, focusing on both its aesthetic shape and its ideological concerns, including important pieces by Sam Schoenbaum (see below), Leeds Barroll on the connection of the play with the Essex rebellion, Cyndia Clegg on the printed play and press censorship, and David Norbrook on the political languages of the play.

Hawkes, Terence. *"Richard II:* The Word Against the Word." *Shakespeare's Talking Animals.* Totowa, N.J.: Rowman and Littlefield, 1974. For Hawkes, the conflict between Richard and Bolingbroke emerges as a conflict between two opposed views of language. Not only do the antagonists use language differently, but each conceives of language in a fundamentally different way: Richard, as a means of changing reality; Bolingbroke, as an arbitrary symbol system expressing merely provisional conceptions of reality.

Hopkins, Lisa. "The King's Melting Body: *Richard II." Companion* to *Shakespeare's Works: The Histories*, ed. Richard Dutton and Jean E. Howard. Oxford: Blackwell, 2003. Hopkins recognizes that the play, even as it carefully locates itself in the ceremonial style of medieval England, carefully uses its self-conscious medievalism to comment on political concerns of late Elizabethan England. More than almost any other history play, *Richard II* frustrates efforts to respond to it as a complete and freestanding account of the events treated (as its gaps and omissions make an audience aware that it is only seeing part of the story), suggesting, Hopkins argues, that it is not intended as an "actual reconstruction of the past, but is in fact fundamentally concerned with the present."

Kantorowicz, Ernst H. "Shakespeare: *King Richard II.*" *The King's Two Bodies: A Study in Medieval Political Theology.* Princeton, N.J.: Princeton Univ. Press, 1957. For Kantorowicz, the play dramatically explores the notion of "the King's two bodies": the belief that the king ruled both in his own person and as a representative of an enduring sacred authority. *Richard II*, he finds, traces the dissolution of the double body: Bolingbroke's ascension to the throne violates the sacramental order and fractures Richard's "twin-born being" as both divine agent and flawed mortal.

Kernan, Alvin B. "The Henriad: Shakespeare's Major History Plays." *Modern Shakespearean Criticism: Essays on Style, Dramaturgy, and the Major Plays*, ed. Alvin B. Kernan. New York: Harcourt, Brace, and World, 1970. Kernan traces the movement of the second tetralogy from a providential view of history in *Richard II* to a pragmatic one in *Henry V*, in which kingship is understood not as a sacramental identity but as a political role. In *Richard II*, as Richard moves from naive confidence in his divine authority to a terrifying awareness of the ambiguity of his position, the play enacts the transition of world views in political and psychological terms.

Mahood, M. M. "*Richard the Second.*" *Shakespeare's Wordplay.* London: Methuen, 1957. For Mahood, *Richard II* is a play that tests the power and efficacy of language. It contrasts the poetic Richard and his faith in words with the politician, Bolingbroke, for whom words have instrumental rather than intrinsic power.

Ornstein, Robert. *"Richard II." A Kingdom for a Stage: The Achievement of Shakespeare's History Plays*. Cambridge: Harvard Univ. Press, 1972. Ornstein focuses on the play's revelation of Richard's self-absorption so that Richard's fall comes to seem both inevitable and appropriate. The play thus raises disturbing questions about political loyalty that are explored dramatically rather than solved ideologically.

Rabkin, Norman. "The Polity." *Shakespeare and the Common Understanding*. New York: Macmillan, Free Press, 1967. Rabkin sees a delicate balance of sympathies as the primary achievement of *Richard II*. Despite the inevitability of Richard's fall from power, our sympathy for him increases with his defeat; and, though Bolingbroke's victory seems politically desirable, we are made fully aware of the moral costs of political success.

Ribner, Irving. *The English History Play in the Age of Shakespeare*, 1957. Rev. ed., enl., New York: Barnes and Noble, 1965, pp. 151–168. For Ribner, *Richard II* is Shakespeare's first great tragedy of character as well as his first great history play. Richard's weaknesses disqualify him for rule, and in Bolingbroke Shakespeare presents an effective if unlawful king to fill the void. England is perhaps better served by Henry than by Richard, but the play measures the sense of human loss in his victory.

Saccio, Peter. "Richard II: The Fall of the King." *Shakespeare's English Kings: History, Chronicle, and Drama*. New York: Oxford Univ. Press, 1977. Using the chronicle accounts of Richard's reign and the research of modern historians to illuminate the background of *Richard II*, Saccio measures the distance between historical fact and Shakespeare's dramatic fiction.

Schoenbaum, S[amuel]. "*Richard II* and the Realities of Power." *Shakespeare Survey* 28 (1975): 1–13. Schoenbaum uses the probable fact of the play's performance on the eve of the Essex Rebellion to explore Shakespeare's own political vision. Shakespeare, he finds, is neither a "seditious playwright" nor the "darling of the court"; rather, he is a "political realist" who unsentimentally understands the realities of power.

Tillyard, E. M. W. "The Second Tetralogy." *Shakespeare's History Plays*, 1944. Rpt., New York: Barnes and Noble, 1964. *Richard II*, in Tillyard's view, is built on the contrast not merely between two characters but between two ways of life: one ceremonial and essentially medieval; the other more vigorous, that of Elizabethan England. Richard, the last king to rule with the full authority of medieval kingship, gives way to Henry, the first to rule outside the sanctions of an authentic succession.

Trousdale, Marion. "The Example of *Richard II*." *Shakespeare and the Rhetoricians*. Chapel Hill, N.C.: Univ. of North Carolina Press, 1982. Considering *Richard II* in the context of Elizabethan rhetorical theory and models, Trousdale finds that the coherence of the play comes not from causal connections between events but from the verbal and structural patterns imposed upon them. Her analysis suggests that the recording of history is less significant than the exploration of the differing ways in which acts and even words may be understood.

Yeats, William Butler. "At Stratford-upon-Avon." *Essays and Introductions*. New York: Macmillan, 1961. Rpt. in part as "*Richard II* and *Henry V*" in *Discussions of Shakespeare's Histories: "Richard II" to "Henry V*," ed. R. J. Dorius. Boston: D. C. Heath, 1964. In response to nineteenth-century condemnation of Richard as sentimental and weak, Yeats argues for Shakespeare's sympathy for him and his poetic nature. In Yeats's view, "Shakespeare cared little for the State," and so Richard's lack of political skill or energy is less telling than his contemplative virtues and the "lyricism which rose out of Richard's mind like the jet of a fountain."

MEMORABLE LINES

The purest treasure mortal times afford
Is spotless reputation.   (MOWBRAY 1.1.177–8)

God's is the quarrel; for God's substitute,
His deputy anointed in His sight,
Hath caused his death; the which if wrongfully
Let heaven revenge, for I may never lift
An angry arm against His minister.   (GAUNT 1.2.37–41)

Truth hath a quiet breast.   (MOWBRAY 1.3.96)

There is no virtue like necessity.   (GAUNT 1.3.278)

Where'er I wander, boast of this I can:
Though banished, yet a trueborn Englishman.
                                (BOLINGBROKE 1.3.308–9)

For violent fires soon burn out themselves.   (GAUNT 2.1.34)

This royal throne of kings, this sceptered isle,
This earth of majesty, this seat of Mars,
This other Eden, demi-paradise,
This fortress built by Nature for herself
Against infection and the hand of war,
This happy breed of men, this little world,
This precious stone set in the silver sea,
Which serves it in the office of a wall
Or as a moat defensive to a house,
Against the envy of less happier lands,
This blessed plot, this earth, this realm, this England . . .
                                (GAUNT 2.1 .40–50)

England, bound in with the triumphant sea,
Whose rocky shore beats back the envious siege
Of wat'ry Neptune . . .   (GAUNT 2.1.61–3)

Take Hereford's rights away, and take from Time
His charters and his customary rights;
Let not tomorrow then ensue today;
Be not thyself; for how art thou a king
But by fair sequence and succession?   (YORK 2.1.195–9)

I count myself in nothing else so happy
As in a soul rememb'ring my good friends.

(BOLINGBROKE 2.3.46–7)

Things past redress are now with me past care.

(YORK 2.3.171)

Eating the bitter bread of banishment . . .

(BOLINGBROKE 3.1.21)

Not all the water in the rough rude sea
Can wash the balm off from an anointed king.

(RICHARD 3.2.54–5)

Oh, call back yesterday, bid time return . . .

(SALISBURY 3.2.69)

Of comfort no man speak!   (RICHARD 3.2.144)

For God's sake, let us sit upon the ground
And tell sad stories of the death of kings.

(RICHARD 3.2.155–6)

I'll give my jewels for a set of beads,
My gorgeous palace for a hermitage,
My gay apparel for an almsman's gown,
My figured goblets for a dish of wood . . .

(RICHARD 3.3.147–50)

I have been studying how I may compare
This prison where I live unto the world.   (RICHARD 5.5.1–2)

I wasted time, and now doth time waste me.

(RICHARD 5.5.49)

Mount, mount, my soul! Thy seat is up on high,
Whilst my gross flesh sinks downward, here to die.

(RICHARD 5.5.111–12)

They love not poison that do poison need.   (KING HENRY 5.6.38)

SEE YOUR BOOKSELLER FOR THESE
BANTAM CLASSICS